神秘王国

古中山国历史文化展

The Mysterious Zhongshan State: Its History and Culture

秦始皇帝陵博物院 编

侯宁彬 主编

西北大学出版社

《神秘王国——古中山国历史文化展》编委会

主　　任　侯宁彬
委　　员（以姓氏笔画为序）
　　　　　　毛保中　田　静　李耀光　杨延临　张　岩　武天新
　　　　　　罗向军　金　岚　周　铁　侯宁彬　侯宏庆　郭向东　徐艳红

主　　编　侯宁彬
副 主 编　郭向东　邵文斌
撰　　文　院长致辞：侯宁彬
　　　　　　学术论文：刘卫华　孔玉倩
　　　　　　正　　文：张　宁　陈　宁
　　　　　　文物信息：李建丽　刘卫华
审　　稿　刘卫华　田旭东
图　　片　张　惠
翻　　译　孔利宁
审　　译　Shiona Airlie
执行编辑　张　宁
图片编辑　赵　震
校　　对　邵文斌　张　宁　叶　晔　付　建（中文）
　　　　　　孔利宁（英文）

展览组织与实施

总 策 划　侯宁彬
项目总监　郭向东
项目负责　邵文斌
内容设计　张　宁
形式设计　蔡一阳
审　　稿　刘卫华　田旭东
图　　片　张　惠
翻　　译　孔利宁
审　　译　Shiona Airlie
展览组织　马生涛　郑　宁　等

目录 Contents

001　院长致辞
　　　Director's Address

003　神秘国度　传奇历史——战国中山国发展史
　　　A History of the Zhongshan State

009　中山国考古
　　　Archaeology of the Zhongshan State

015　序言
　　　Foreword

017　第一部分　鲜虞中山
　　　Foundation of the Zhongshan State

041　第二部分　国都灵寿
　　　Lingshou as the Capital

069　第三部分　社会生活
　　　Social Life of the State

109　第四部分　田猎兵事
　　　Hunting and Military Affairs

161　第五部分　中山王陵
　　　Mausoleum of the Kings of the Zhongshan State

212　附录：『神秘王国——古中山国历史文化展』展览设计图
　　　Renderings of the Exhibition "The Mysterious Zhongshan State: Its History and Culture"

217　后记
　　　Postscript

神秘王国——古中山国历史文化展

院长致辞

春秋战国是中国历史上的第一个大变革时期，同时也是中华大地文化交融、思想碰撞最为活跃的阶段。在那个风云际会的时代，各方势力为图存争霸而相互征伐，先后涌现出了以春秋五霸、战国七雄为代表的强盛诸侯国，同时还有诸多实力相对弱小的诸侯国，他们为了自己的生存发展而纵横捭阖，厮杀疆场，在春秋战国的历史画卷上也留下了自己浓墨重彩的一笔。

中山国就是这样一个充满神秘色彩的小诸侯国。中山国始建于周景王初年（前544—前533年），最初称作鲜虞，中山文公时（前459—前414年）改称中山。前后立国二百余年，经略五百余里（今河北省石家庄市与保定市之间），战国中期达到鼎盛，是仅次于齐、楚、燕、韩、赵、魏、秦七国的一个较强的"千乘之国"。

中山国由小到大，几次被强国所灭，但它虽灭未亡，又几度复国。经过历代国君励精图治，中山国在夹缝中求得生存，不断强大，最终于公元前323年与魏国、韩国、赵国、燕国共同称王，国力达到巅峰。

中山国的历史虽然跌宕起伏、波澜壮阔，但是在中国史学权威著作《史记》中却没有关于中山国历史和王系的专篇记载或记述，全书虽然多次提及中山国，却多为陪衬，仅一笔带过。史料的大量缺失使这个"千乘之国"湮没于历史的尘埃之中，充满了神秘色彩。

二十世纪七八十年代，考古工作者对战国中山国都城——灵寿古城和中山王陵进行了系统的考古调查和发掘，出土了数以万计的具有重要历史价值、艺术价值的珍贵文物。这也让人们将视线再次聚焦于2000多年前这个曾经存国200多年的神秘王国——中山国。发掘出土的中山王䰉（cuò）铁足大铜鼎、夔龙纹方壶、妤蛮（zǐ zǐ）铜圆壶等文物分别刻有469字、450字和204字铭文，记载了中山王世系和中山国历史上的重大事件，以有力的实物资料，弥补了中山国史料记载的缺失。

为了展现中山国历史文化，展示中山国考古研究综合成果，秦始皇帝陵博物院在河北省文物局、陕西省文物局、河北省博物院、河北省文物研究所的大力支持下，策划了"神秘王国——古中山国历史文化展"，这是秦始皇帝陵博物院"东周时期地域文化系列展"的又一力作。

此次展览将展出中山国的110组（239件）精美文物，材质上有金、银、铜、玉、陶等，工艺上匠心独具、精美绝伦。彰显王权至上的青铜重器、奇巧瑰丽的生活用器、晶莹剔透的精美玉器、细致精巧的黑陶明器、造型独特的人物和动物圆雕艺术品……许多的器物都与中原艺术品风格迥异，展现了中山国人充满神秘幻想的意境和蓬勃向上的活力，将中山国的历史面貌和风土人情生动地展示于世人面前。

为了让这些精美而蕴涵历史文化信息的文物在展览之外能够发挥更好的鉴赏、传播、交流和研究的作用，秦始皇帝陵博物院特意编写出版了该展览的同名图录。在图录编写过程中，我们不仅选取了展览中的所有展品，还精心挑选了未能参加展出的代表中山文化的近20件文物，以充分展示中山国的考古研究成果及其历史文化面貌。希望这本图录的出版，能够成为展览的有益补充，能够为中山国的历史学与考古学研究提供图文资料，能够为东周区域文化系列的比较研究增加新的内容与视角。

侯宁彬

2017年6月

神秘国度　传奇历史
——战国中山国发展史

河北博物院 研究员 刘卫华

战国时期，"万乘之国七[1]，千乘之国五。"[2]中山国跻身十二强国。但由于中山国统治者非周王室宗亲且国运几经起伏等原因，史书对中山国的记载简略而零散，其遗物、遗迹又长期湮没于地下，所以在长达两千多年的时间里中山国成为鲜为人知的"神秘王国"。二十世纪七十年代以来，考古工作者在河北省平山县三汲乡一带发掘了中山国都灵寿古城和五座中山王族墓及大量平民墓，共出土文物两万余件，使中山雄风再现于世。

群雄争霸的战国时代，中山国特别善于利用大国之间的矛盾，在列强的夹缝中开疆拓土，其发展历史跌宕起伏，充满传奇色彩。

一、扑朔迷离的发展起源

中山国曲折的历史留下了很多谜团，关于其族属、姓氏及发展历程等问题历来众说纷纭，争论的焦点集中在中山国的族属与起源、"鲜虞"与"中山"的关系。争论主要有以下两种观点：

第一种，少数学者认为，中山是由春秋时期活跃在太行山麓滹沱河一带的鲜虞国更名而来的，其主要文献依据是《汉书·地理志》注引应劭云："新市（今正定县新城铺一带），本鲜于[3]子国，今鲜虞亭是也。"司马彪《续汉书·郡国志》中山国新市条记载："有鲜虞亭，故国，子姓。"1977年天津武清出土的东汉《鲜于璜碑》中说鲜于璜为殷"箕子之苗裔"，由此认为中山国是由子姓鲜虞发展而来。但罗泌撰《路史》载："鲜虞·续志云：子姓国，鲜虞子，中山新市也。有鲜虞故城，白狄别居，种最大，晋伐之。"又称子姓鲜虞为白狄别种，从而为这一学说增加了模棱两可之处。

第二种，多数学者认为，中山国是由狄族东迁而来，而且认为其源于白狄、长狄、众狄的学者都有。春秋时期，居住于我国北方和西方的民族被统称为"狄族"或"戎族"，狄族又分为赤狄、白狄和长狄几支。其中的白狄，春秋前期主要生活在今陕北高原和晋陕交界处，与秦国、晋国的联系比较密切。《世本》记载"鲜虞，姬姓，白狄也"。杜预《春秋经传集解》中记"鲜虞，白狄别种，在中山新市县[4]"，其《春秋释例》又进一步说明鲜虞为姬姓白狄。唐初杨士勋《春秋谷梁传疏》云:"鲜虞,姬姓,白狄也者,《世本》文也。"多数学者承袭以上记载中的观点,认为鲜虞属于白狄族的一支。原中山国境内发现的一些积石墓及墓中出土的金丝圈耳环、虎形金饰片、绿松石饰品、矮柄釜形豆、提梁铜匏壶、提链铜壶等,也确实显示出北方游牧民族的风格。[5]

春秋时期,白狄在陕北过着游牧生活,屡屡南下侵犯相邻的秦国、晋国,且时而倒向晋,时而倒向秦。《国语·郑语》记载,公元前774年,郑桓公问史伯何处才能安居,史伯说,在洛阳王城以北除有燕、卫等诸侯之外,还有"狄、鲜虞、潞、洛、泉、徐、蒲",这是"鲜虞"之名首见于史书记载。

春秋中叶,受到秦国的挤压,以及晋国和戎政策的诱惑,白狄部向东迁徙,经晋北出太行山,在太行山东麓的滹沱河[6]流域一带定居。《春秋》记"(襄公)十八年(公元前555年)春,白狄始来。"在山西境内滹沱河流域的原平及其周边的代县、定襄发现的一批春秋晚期至战国早期墓葬,与河北平山中山国墓葬的出土文物有类似之处,可考证中山的东迁路线。[7]

那么白狄鲜虞部又是如何变身中山国的呢?以何直刚、田卫平等为代表的学者认为,鲜虞与中山没有关系,鲜虞与中山不是一脉相传、前后相继的部族或国家,不是一国,也不是一族。以李学勤、段连勤等为代表的多数学者认为鲜虞为战国中山的前身。这一学说中,又有一族二统说,认为鲜虞与中山属于同族,但是君统不相继。

由于史料记载的简略,鲜虞与中山的关系确实有含混的一面,这也是很多学者正在研究探讨的一个问题。东晋范宁《春秋谷梁传注疏》曰:"鲜虞,姬姓,白狄也,地居中山。"据一些文献资料中所记有关中山国的史实,可以看出鲜虞与中山前后相继的脉络。目前因为没有其它更明确的证据,所以多数学者依现有史料比较认同鲜虞即中山前身的说法。

《左传》记:"(定公)四年(公元前506年)春三月,刘文公合诸侯于召陵,谋伐楚也。晋荀寅求货于蔡侯,弗得,言于范献子曰:'国家方危,诸侯方贰,将以袭敌,不亦难乎。水潦方降,疾疟方起,中山不服。弃盟取怨,无损于楚,而失中山。不如辞蔡侯。'"这是"中山"作为国号首次出现于《左传》之中,杜预《春秋左传集解》认为:"中山,鲜虞。"多数学者同意这个解释,认为此"中山"即指"鲜虞"。

二、中山国与晋国的关系

春秋末期到战国初期,白狄部与晋国的纠葛最多。白狄与晋国的关系曾经一度比较密切,"重耳奔狄"即是证明。晋献公之骊姬陷害太子申生和重耳、夷吾兄弟,重耳因母亲狐姬是狄人,所以流亡白狄达12年之久,娶狄女季隗并生下儿子。公元前636年,秦穆公送重耳回晋,立为晋文公,晋文公时,晋与白狄结盟。

公元前628年,晋文公去世,其与齐女所生的晋襄公继位。白狄君企图送晋文公在狄所生之子回到晋国争位。《春秋》记载,公元前627年,白狄到达箕[8]时,晋军"败狄于箕。郤缺获白狄子"。

《左传》昭公十二年(公元前530年)记:"晋伐鲜虞",又记:"晋荀吴伪会齐师者,假道于鲜虞。"说明春秋后期,白狄鲜虞已由陕西、山西东迁到河北。东迁后的白狄主要由鲜虞氏、肥氏、鼓氏、仇由氏四个部族组成,其它三部先后为晋所灭,只有鲜虞部留存下来,并不断进行扩张,在史书中被兼称"鲜虞"或"中山"。

在与中原各国的竞争中,鲜虞中山国的命运几经波折,并一度介入晋国统治集团的内乱。公元前494年，中山与齐、卫共同伐晋，取得晋国的棘蒲[9]。公元前491年，晋大夫中行寅因晋国内乱逃奔中山，中山国将他接纳到新占领的柏人[10]。于是，晋国于公元前489年派赵鞅"帅师伐鲜虞"，大破中山，此后二十余年间史籍对中山国都没有只字记载。公元前457年，中山国又遭到晋国的致命打击，一直销声匿迹了四十多年。

三、文公、武公重创基业

公元前455—公元前453年，晋国智伯水灌晋阳城，韩、魏、赵三家灭智氏，分晋国。中山国乘机崛起。这一时期，领导中山国重新兴起的应该是中山文公。中山王刻铭铜方壶铭文上，明确刻有"隹朕皇祖文武，（桓）祖成考"的字样，证明文公是战国中山国的创立者，他的时代也是扑朔迷离的鲜虞中山与战国中山分野的时代。但是关于文公，史书上并没有记载，从铜方壶铭文上才了解到他的存在。

中山文公之后，是中山武公。《史记·赵世家》记载："（赵献侯十年，公元前414年）中山武公初立。"《世本·居篇》记载："中山武公居顾，桓公徙灵寿。"

中山武公复国，即是利用了周围几个大国忙于战争，无暇顾及中山的时机。公元前419至公元前408年，魏国同秦国争夺河西之地；"前415年（晋烈公元年）晋赵浣（赵献子）城泫氏[11]。韩启章（韩武子）都平阳[12]。"[13]于是武公趁机开疆扩土，并建都于顾。《太平寰宇记》引《九州要记》曰："唐县，本白狄种，最为夷狄大国，梁开平三年改为中山县。"在今河北唐县北城子、西城子一带发现有大规模城址遗址和墓葬，推测即为当时顾的旧地。武公仿效华夏诸国建立政治、军事制度，中山国迎来了又一次发展机遇。文公和武公在铜方壶铭文中被尊为"皇祖文武"。

四、桓公与成公的中兴

武公复兴中山后不久就去世了，继位的桓公尚且年幼。而此时，想称霸中原的魏文侯正对中山国虎视眈眈。公元前408年，魏国刚刚夺取河西之地，魏文侯就派乐羊借道赵国，进军中山。中山国君派正在中山居住的乐羊之子乐舒劝说乐羊退兵，劝说无效后就将乐舒做成肉羹给乐羊送去。《战国策》记载："乐羊坐于幕下而啜之，尽一杯。"此事更加激怒了乐羊，他带兵猛攻中山，"三年而拔之"[14]，使中山成为魏国的附庸。

"中山，魏虽灭之，尚不绝祀"[15]，大概是一定程度上保留了中山国君的宗庙和公室。公元前383至公元前381年，赵、楚和魏、卫之间连年征战，魏国大败，中山桓公趁机复国。桓公复国的时间，史籍缺乏明确记载，学者们推断约在公元前380年前后。桓公建立的新都——灵寿古城，位于今平山县三汲乡一带。古城西北傍太行山，南依滹沱河，东临华北平原，地理位置优越。

建都灵寿古城后约四十年，中山桓公去世，其子成公继续富国强兵，中山王𰯼铁足铜鼎记载："昔者吾先祖桓王，邵考成王，身勤社稷，行四方，以忧劳邦家。"铭文中追称桓公、成公为王，并颂扬了他们勤于治国的业绩。

成公时期，中山曾经"引水围鄗[16]"。公元前332年，齐、魏共同伐赵，中山国乘机决槐水围困赵国的鄗邑，直到齐、魏撤军，才解除了围困。这件事对赵国的触动非常大，赵武灵王在劝说公子成接受胡服骑射时就说："先时中山负齐之强兵，侵暴吾地，系累吾民，引水围鄗……今骑射之备，近可以便上党之形，而远可以报中山之怨。"[17] "引水围鄗"成为激发赵武灵王实行"胡服骑射"改革的重要原因。

五、王䪨时期达于鼎盛

成公去逝后，新君䪨继位。䪨是中山最鼎盛时期的国君，国家日益强盛，国土不断增大，在群雄间纵横捭阖。䪨的国君之路并不是一帆风顺的，铁足铜鼎铭文中回顾了他的成长经历："昔者，吾先考成王，早弃群臣，寡人幼童未通智，佳傅姆是从。"成公去世时䪨的年龄应该不超过十岁，幸有司马相邦的教导与辅佐。司马相邦是中山国历史上的一位重要人物，辅佐了成公、䪨和㜏蚉三代国君，在"中山三器"铭文中被反复提及。在司马相邦的教导和辅佐下，䪨一步步成长起来，中山国国力达于鼎盛，经济繁荣，军事强大，成为千乘之国，与韩、魏、燕、赵共同称王，史称"五国相王"。公元前323年，魏惠王采纳公孙衍的建议，联合韩、赵、燕、中山几个国家共同称王，一起对抗秦国。在共同称王的这几个国家里，中山是最弱小的，齐威王对此表示强烈反对。于是，中山便派足智多谋的臣子张登在齐、燕、赵等各国之间奔走游说，最后各国都同意中山国称王，䪨成为中山国历史上第一位称王的国君。

称王之后，中山国又遇到了一个趁火打劫的好机会。公元前321年，燕易王去世，燕王哙继位，后把王位让给了相国子之，太子平等贵族对此强烈不满并聚众攻打子之，引发"子之之乱"。燕国内乱，齐国以平乱为名，攻入燕国。中山国见有机可乘，也派大军攻打燕国，"列城数十，克敌大邦"，还掠夺了大量青铜器。据铜方壶铭文记载，此壶系中山伐燕胜利后，"择燕吉金，铸为彝壶"，铁足铜鼎和㜏蚉铜圆壶铭文也都对中山伐燕作了大篇幅的记述。

伐燕胜利后，中山国的国势达到了顶峰，"错处六国之间，纵横捭阖，交相控引，争衡天下"[18]。

六、中山国兴亡的启示

中山国处于春秋战国乱世，屡次被灭，又屡次复国。这个小国为什么能够一再从绝境中复兴，并一度兴旺发达呢？从总体上看，中山国有以下几点优势：

第一，地理位置优越。中山国位于太行山麓东侧一带，西倚太行山，扼冀晋之咽喉，东临华北平原，地理位置十分优越，发展农牧业生产的自然资源都很丰富。

第二，善于兼收并包。中山国虽然具有游牧民族传统，但进入中原地区后，积极吸收华夏文化，"中山三器"铭文中有大量对华夏文化典籍的引用，多处表现出对儒家学说的宣扬，铭文的文学造诣很高，表现出中山国对华夏经典的深度吸收。

第三，注意发展经济。中山国交通发达，境内横贯东西的道路是联结太行山东西两侧的纽带，陆路交通南接邯郸，北通燕涿，东到临淄，西北可到代国。中山境内河流众多，水运发达。《史记》中称中山人"仰机利而食"，商业活动相当普遍。中山以"多美物"著称，制陶业、制玉业、铜铁冶铸业均具有很高的工艺水平。另外，中山国统治者认识到"作敛中则庶民附"[19]，注意减轻农民负担，调动其积极性。

第四，具有游牧雄风。中山人喜猎、尚武，兵强马壮，武备精良，战车轻便灵活，木皮铁杖等杀伤力强，而且中山人具有威猛善战的雄风和不屈不挠的精神，所以能屡克劲敌，跻身强国之列。

第五，善于利用大国矛盾。春秋战国时期列国纷争，中山国善于利用强国之间的矛盾，争取时机，不断发展壮大，一次次死而复生，落而后起。

𧊒在位时中山国曾称雄一时，那么为什么又很快灭亡了呢？中山国表面的强盛下，其实隐藏着深刻的危机，大臣弄权、政治腐败、外交失当、享乐成风、国贫兵弱、内外交困，终被赵国所灭。具体原因主要有：

第一，民风败坏。中山国因具有游牧民族传统，因此保留了部分粗野民俗，"中山之俗，以昼为夜，以夜继日，男女切倚，固无休息，康乐歌谣好悲，其主弗知恶，此亡国之风也。"[20] 另外，"中山地薄人众，犹有沙丘纣淫地余民，民俗懁急，仰机利而食。丈夫相聚游戏，悲歌慷慨，起则相随椎剽，休则掘冢，作巧奸冶，多美物，为倡优。女子则鼓鸣瑟，跕屣，游媚贵富，入后宫，遍诸侯。"[21]《吕氏春秋·先识篇》也记载："白圭至中山，中山之王欲留之，白圭固辞，乘舆而去；又之齐，齐王欲留之，仕又辞而去。人问其故。曰：'之二国者皆将亡。所学有五尽，何谓五尽？'曰：'莫之必则信尽矣，莫之誉则名尽矣，莫之爱则亲尽矣，行者无粮、居者无食则财尽矣，不能用人，又不能自用则功尽矣。国有此五者，无幸必亡。中山、齐皆当此。'"以上记载均说明，中山国民风粗野，喜好享乐，不重礼义，声名丧尽。

第二，政治腐败。中山国国君治国不明，偏听偏信。《战国策》记载："中山有贱公子，马甚瘦，车甚弊。左右有私不善者，乃为之请王曰：'公子甚贫，马甚瘦，王何不益之马食？'王不许。左右因微令夜烧刍厩。王以为贱公子也，乃诛之。"另有一篇记："季辛与爰骞相怨。司马喜新与季辛恶，因微令人杀爰骞，中山之君以为季辛也，因诛之。"以上两段文字，说明中山国君断事不明、处事昏庸，也助长了大臣间的相互猜忌与陷害之风。

第三，忽视军备与生产。中山国在吸收华夏文明的过程中表现出了对儒学极大的尊崇，曾一度"伉礼下布衣之士以百数矣"；在"中山三器"铭文中，也多处表现出对仁义、尊贤、爱民等儒学思想的宣扬。战国时期群雄争霸，各国都在奖励耕战，中山国片面强调"贵儒学，贱壮士"[22]的政策，导致"战士惰于行阵""农夫惰于田"，造成"兵弱于敌，国贫于内"的局面。

第四，外交失当。中山国国运曲折，历经风雨，战乱不断，因其特殊的国情与经历，中山国形成了趋利避害的实用主义外交方针，结果导致四面树敌，与多数大国结怨。魏国曾灭过中山国；齐国在中山称王时接连被说客张登蒙骗；燕国的"子之之乱"，中山趁火打劫；赵国更是将中山视为心腹大患。

公元前307年，赵国发动对中山国的进攻，中山国进行了苦苦抵抗。"赵氏攻中山。中山之人多力者，曰吾丘鸩，衣铁甲，操铁杖以战，而所击无不碎，所冲无不陷，以车投车，以人投人也。"[23] 中山拼死抵抗之时，齐、魏、燕等大国都袖手旁观，中山国孤立无援。

公元前296年，赵国攻灭中山国都，国君姿蚤逃往齐国，赵国扶立尚为傀儡国君，一年后将其迁往肤施（今陕西榆林一带），中山国彻底灭亡。

注释：

1. [汉]刘向著，缪文远、罗永莲、缪伟译注：《战国策》，中华书局，2016年。
2. "万乘之国七"指秦、齐、楚、燕、赵、魏、韩；"千乘之国五"说法不一，一说为宋、鲁、卫、郑、中山。
3. "于"为"虞"之假借。
4. 今河北正定县新城铺一带。
5. 杨建华：《白狄东迁考》，转自《鄂尔多斯青铜器国际学术研讨论文集》，科学出版社，2009年。
6. 即古代的鲜虞水。
7. 杨建华：《白狄东迁考》，转自《鄂尔多斯青铜器国际学术研讨论文集》，科学出版社，2009年。
8. 今山西蒲县东北。
9. 今河北赵县。
10. 今河北内丘东北。
11. 今山西高平。
12. 今山西临汾西南。
13. [汉]皇甫谧著，陆吉等点校：《帝王世纪·世本·逸周书·古本行书纪年》，齐鲁书社，2010年。
14. [汉]刘向著，缪文远、罗永莲、缪伟译注：《战国策》，中华书局，2016年。
15. [汉]司马迁著：《史记》，中华书局，1982年。
16. 今河北高邑县境内。
17. [汉]司马迁著：《史记》，中华书局，1982年。
18. [清]王先谦撰：《鲜虞中山国事表·疆域图说》，广文书局，1978年。
19. 中山王刻铭铜方壶铭文。
20. 许维遹撰：《吕氏春秋集释》，中华书局，2009年。
21. [汉]司马迁著：《史记》，中华书局，1982年。
22. [宋]乐史撰，王文楚等点校：《太平寰宇记》，中华书局，2007年。
23. 许维遹撰：《吕氏春秋集释》，中华书局，2009年。

中山国考古

河北省文物研究所 副研究员 孔玉倩

二十世纪七十年代中后期，河北省平山县三汲村，这个地处太行山东麓滹沱河北岸的一个默默无名的小村庄，因为一个惊天大发现而一夜之间蜚声中外。考古工作者经过数年艰辛而缜密的发掘，深埋于地下两千多年的战国时期中山国都城及王墓被发现，这一重大发现开启了中国东周考古的新篇章。

一、中山国简史

中山国是战国时期北方少数民族狄族的鲜虞部落建立的一个诸侯国，位于今河北省的中部、太行山东麓一带。因为城中有山，故而得名。

早在春秋时期，这支姬姓白狄族就已经建立了国家，先称鲜虞，后又改为中山，但究竟何时改名，并不见于史册。而"中山"这一名字，最早见于《左传·定公四年》（公元前506年）记载，杜预注云："中山，鲜虞。"这一记载之前，翻检史籍只有"鲜虞"这个称呼。此后"鲜虞""中山"则兼而称之。另据考证，"鲜虞"这一称谓止于鲁哀公六年（公元前489年），此后则均以"中山"之名而载入史册。但是也有一个例外，那就是公元前457年，赵襄子占左人、中人，用伐"狄"来记述。由此也可以看出，"中山国"的历史地位至此已为历史所公认，而此时，按中山国的王系来推算应当在中山文公之时。

鲜虞在列强纷争中逐渐兴起，并开始仿效华夏诸国建立国家。据《史记》记载："赵献侯十年（公元前414年），中山武公初立，居顾（今定州市），桓公徙灵寿。"中山武公是文公的儿子，在他执政之时，率领人们离开贫瘠闭塞的山区，放弃当年被晋国占领军毁灭的都城，向东部广阔肥沃的平原迁徙，在顾建立了新都。新都初成，年轻英武的中山武公，以不甘平庸，想要有所建树的姿态，依照华夏诸国奉行的礼制，建立了一套中山国的政治、军事制度，对国家完成了初步的治理和规划。但是好景不长，内忧和外患同时困扰着年轻的中山国，可叹一身抱负的武公迁都不久便离开人世。其子桓公即位,又将都城从顾迁至太行山东麓的灵寿(在今平山县三汲乡,东距今灵寿县城约10千米)。

春秋战国时期,在我国历史上既是列强争战、相互兼并的时代,也是各个民族大融合的时代,早期鲜虞中山国的形成和发展便证实了这一点。地处民族杂处中心地区之一的山西、河北,也是古代北方民族融合的中心,狄族在与华夏族的交往中,不断地吸收农业民族的先进生产方式和文化习俗,但在某些方面仍顽强地保留着本民族的一些落后习俗。《吕氏春秋·先识》中说:"中山之俗,以昼为夜,以夜继日,男女切倚,固无休息,康乐歌谣好悲,其主弗知恶,此亡国之风也。"这种落后的习俗,严重地削弱了战斗力,直接影响国力的增长,甚至陷于亡国的绝境。而年幼的桓公继承王位后却并没有意识到形势的严峻,由于"不恤国政",加上当时周边大国的不断进攻,公元前407年,中山国被"七雄"之一的魏国所灭,成为魏的属国,长达二十余年。魏在执政期间,施行怀柔政策,带来了先进的中原文化,客观上推动了中山国经济、文化等方面的巨大发展。

公元前380年前后,桓公经过二十余年的励精图志,中山国再度崛起,仍定都灵寿。随着国势日渐增强,由于中山国毗邻赵国,逐渐成为赵国的心腹之患。灵寿城,是中山国后期,桓公自顾迁此建立的都城,不久便被魏占领。复国后的中山国,桓公仍以此为都。灵寿城地理位置优越,西倚太行山,南临滹沱河,向东是开阔的冲积平原,土地肥沃,林木繁茂,既便于防守,也便于经济的发展,是个休养生息的绝佳之地。

中山复国后,共立五代,分别为桓公、成公、王𧵽、王䤿䧅、王尚。其中中山桓公、成公均是有所作为的君主,他们在政治、经济乃至城市规划、建设上都大量吸收和借鉴先进的中原文化。在全国除经营传统的畜牧经济外,还大力发展农耕经济。从考古资料看,铁农具的种类和数量都有不少增加和变化。到了王𧵽(前327—前313年)统治时期,选贤举能,任用老臣司马赒为相,修缮武备,扩充军队,使国力猛增,拥有战车千辆,兵甲过万,达到中山有史以来的鼎盛期。国力的强盛,使中山国一度可与燕、赵、齐、楚、魏、韩、秦分庭抗礼,成为仅次于"战国七雄"的"千乘之国"。特别是在公元前323年,中山国参与了和赵、燕、魏、韩结盟共同对抗秦、齐、楚的"五国相王"运动,更是显赫一时。公元前314年,又与齐共同伐燕,掠夺了燕的大批财物和土地,取得辉煌战果。虽为"千乘之国",却能长期纵横捭阖于大国之间,在战国史上占有不可或缺的地位。王𧵽死后,继位的䤿䧅由于内政外交政策措施不当,使中山国内外交困,国力日衰,公元前296年,终被强大的赵国所灭,王䤿䧅仓皇出逃到齐国。赵国立年幼的王尚为傀儡国王,第二年,又将王尚迁到肤施(今陕西榆林一带),一代强国中山至此宣告灭亡。

二、发现之旅

灭亡后的中山国从此销声匿迹,沉寂两千多年而不为人所知。时间追溯到1935年春夏之交,在平山县南中七汲村偶然发现一块刻有文字的光滑的石头,上有"监罟"和"守丘"等文字,联系史籍,有人推断战国中山王的池罟和陵墓就在附近,可以说为中山王墓的发现与发掘提供了线索。转眼二十多年过去了,1956年在三汲乡又发现了一些战国时期的青铜车器。而从20世纪70年代起,陆续发现了许多春秋和战国时期的墓葬内的铜器、金丝圈和金虎形饰等随葬物品,其器形同常见的燕国、赵国的器物不尽相同,引起了考古工作者的注意。1973年冬,为了平沟垫地建农场，三汲乡准备于中七汲村西 1.5 千米高地 "陵台"上取土，于是报请省文化局批准，河北省文物管理处遂派两名干部到现场配合这次冬季取土工程。1974 年，当地刘杨村农民将挖渠中发现的战国时期铜器和玛瑙环送交文物管理处。文物管理处即派人到现场做了认真调查并对相关墓葬进行了清理。通过调查了解到三汲乡一带，不但有春秋战国时期的一般墓群，而且还有保存高大封土，相当于国王级的陵墓。另外，调查中还发现地面上散布着大量战国时期的陶片，同时还暴露有窑址和夯土层等，这种种迹象说明这里还存在有战国时代的遗址。特别是中七汲村西高地上东西并列的两座"陵台"令人充满期待。而这两座墓就是 1973 年冬文化局批准取土的两座"陵台"，此时北半部已被严重破坏。台上出土许多战国时期的筒瓦、板瓦和柱石，说明封土中应有建筑遗迹。这一切都引起考古工作者的思考，大家反复揣摩着这一带出土的这些具有明显北方民族文化特点的遗物，又联系到战国时期中山国后期建都于灵寿这一史实，大胆推测两座陵台下的墓应是中山国境域内的国王级陵墓。正是在这一充满诱惑和挑战的驱使下，考古工作者展开全面的调查，进而实施科学的考古发掘，而最终使当时的推测得到了完美的印证。战国中山国都城——灵寿古城址和战国中山王墓及其陪葬墓均被发现，神秘王国的面纱一步步揭开，从此中山国的历史、文化、艺术等方面的研究翻开了崭新的一页。

三、考古揭秘

中山国灵寿故城址和王陵区的发掘，使人们第一次直观地、近距离地认识了中山国。

（一）灵寿都城址

公元前 380 年左右，中山复国，迁都灵寿，公元前 296 年，赵灭中山。灵寿为都达 80 余年。城址地处太行山东麓，北依东陵山，南临滹沱河，倚山面水，位置优越。全城包括主城区和东侧的附属城堡两大部分。主城依天然地势而建，平面呈不规则形。城址遭到严重破坏，只残存部分城垣。城垣夯筑，南部狭窄，北部宽阔，东西最宽约 4000 米，南北最长处约 4500 米，城内地势北高南低。中间有一道南北走向的夯筑城垣把城分为东城、西城两部分。城垣外侧以天然河道构成护城壕沟。考古发现证实东城主要是宫殿区和作坊区，城内中部南北一线分布着大型夯筑建筑基址群，城内中西部则分布着制陶、铸铜和铸铁等手工业作坊区和普通民宅，城内北部中央有座小山；西城中部以一道隔墙将城分为南北两个区。北区为王陵区，南区为手工业作坊和普通居住区。附属城堡平面呈长方形，城内中部发现一方形宫殿类夯土建筑基址，该城堡应与军事有关。多年的考古发现还证实城外近郊分布着多处平民墓地，而城西南远郊还发现了分布密集的祭祀坑，这是灵寿城为都前已得到相当发展的证明。灵寿城是我国战国时多城组团式格局的代表，也是因地制宜建城的典范。

（二）中山王𰯼墓

在灵寿城营建的过程中，就将西城北区规划为单纯的王陵园区，占据了优越的地理位置，这是战国城址中所不多见的。检索文献记载，中山复国后五位国君中的三位葬于此。城内西北部由东北向西南排列两座王陵，南面一座编号为 M6，其西侧有三座中型墓，编号分别为 M3、M4、M5。城外西约 2 千米的岗坡地上，由西而东并列两座大墓，编号为 M1、M2。除 M5 外，其它几座墓葬均有陪葬墓。1974—1978 年，河北省文物研究所发掘了其中的 M1、M6 两座大墓，根据对墓葬形制和出土器物的研究，获知 M1 为中山王䂮墓，M2 应为哀后墓，M6 为中山成公墓，M7 为中山桓公墓。

中山王䂮墓（M1）是已发掘的中山国王墓葬中规模最大、保存最好的一座。墓上有用黄褐色粘土夯筑而成的高大封土堆，形似金字塔形，虽因取土被严重破坏，但残高仍达 15 米，顶部长宽为 18 米，底边东西约 90 米，南北 100.5 米。封土的平面为方形，呈三级台阶状。南面有宽阔的平台。封土的第二层台阶上，残存着回廊建筑遗迹，推测应是一座周绕回廊、上覆瓦顶的三层台榭式建筑。第一层台阶的北面有五座陪葬墓，封土下也有一座陪葬墓。南面东西两侧各有车马坑一座，西侧车马坑西面并排有杂殉坑一座、葬船坑一座。

中山王䂮墓高大封土覆压之下的是墓室。墓室平面呈中字形，南北各有一条墓道，通长 97 米、宽 30 米、高 5.6—5.7 米。墓葬由墓道和椁室两部分组成。地上墓道部分规模较大，夯筑而成，高 5.6—5.7 米，其外沿部分与墓丘平台连成一体。椁室位于墓葬中部，平面呈亚字形，由于曾被盗掘和火烧，棺椁和其它木质的东西都已不存，只残存一些金属物品。从残破的铜饰判断，中山王䂮死后采用二棺二椁四层棺椁入葬。

䂮墓最引人注目的特点是墓室内椁室的东、西、东北部分别有三个暗藏珍宝的"库"，这在战国大墓中也是不多见的。三个库由于和椁室不相通，没有被盗墓者发现，因而没有被盗掘，除东北库没有随葬品外，其它两个库都出土了大量珍贵文物，许多闻名中外的精美器物就出于此，如著名的中山舒蚉圆壶、错金银四龙四凤铜方案、错金银虎噬鹿铜屏风座、错金银铜犀屏风座和牛错金银铜屏风座、十五连盏铜灯、三犀足铜筒形器、鹰柱铜盘等均出于东库。中山王䂮九鼎、中山王䂮铜方壶、铜编钟及 350 余件精美的大器均出土于西库。

两座车马坑的大小、形状基本相同。坑内用木板墙隔开而分成南北两部分，南部葬马，北部葬车。一号车马坑盗掘严重，遗物和遗迹已寥寥无几，只有南部残留马骨架 12 具；二号车马坑北部放置有铜山字形器 5 件、马车 4 辆，4 辆车上均配有各式兵器，南面有 12 具马骨架。

杂殉坑平面呈长方形，南北长，东西宽，它的形制与二号车马坑基本相同，也分为南北两部分，南部葬羊和马，北部葬车、帐、狗等，这些都是墓主人生前狩猎所用物品。由于盗掘，残存的物品很少，出土有一件帐篷中心铜柱帽、一些小件车器以及动物骨架，其中一对狗骨架颈部戴有用金银片制成的扁管状项圈，推测应该是国王最钟爱的一对犬。

另有一坑位于杂殉坑的西面，位置比较低，推测可能和水中行船有关。由于遭到严重盗掘，坑内的遗物所剩无几。坑分南北二室，放置着不同种类的木船。从遗迹来看，南室原来应该并排放着三条大船，三船在后部三分之一处并联，在船板上还发现有编钟、石磬、鼓等娱乐工具，推测主要是供国王游玩行乐时使用。北室仅放置一条船，应为主船，上面装饰彩色的图画，显得富丽华美。

（三）中山成公墓

中山成公墓(M6)与䂮墓形制相仿，只是规模稍小。平面也呈"中"字形，内填有积石、积炭。墓室、墓道通长 91 米，宽 27.5 米。封土和墓室均遭到严重破坏。封土下西侧靠北有两座陪葬墓，东侧相应位置有一座陪葬墓。南面墓道的东西两侧各有一个车马坑。

墓室同样分地上和地下两个部分。地下部分中心为椁室，平面近似长方形，因为被盗及墓葬坍陷，几乎没有出土随葬的器物。

椁室的东西两边分别是东库和西库，形制基本一致，平面口部呈长方形。东库南北长 4.1 米、东西宽 2.48 米、深 2.1 米，库内存有木椁，已完全腐朽，但依稀可辨当初的彩绘痕迹，库内出土铜山字形器、一组陶礼器和漆器，还发现了狩猎用的皮帐。西库南北长 4.05 米、宽 2.44 米、深 2.2 米，同样葬有彩绘的木椁。出土了与东库山字形器配套使用的半个铜山字形器和代表王权的铜九鼎、羞鼎、人俑灯等，以及一组取暖工具，包括铜双提链耳三足盆、有柄箕、五齿小耙等。而东西库出土的皮帐和帐内取暖工具在河北省是第一次发现。

中山国考古的惊天大发现，让一个神秘的王国揭开了面纱，一座气势恢弘的城池，一件件巧构奇思的文物，无不让人流连忘返、回味无穷。中山国考古的重大发现也为华夏文明的长河增添了一抹瑰丽璀璨的色彩。

Foreword

The Zhongshan State was once one of the most important states in ancient China during the Warring States Period because of its strong military forces, which included at least 1,000 war chariots in its army. Equal to the other seven leading states at that time, it was founded by the nomadic Xianyu tribe of the Baidi people. The Zhongshan State had a relatively short history and so is hardly mentioned in Chinese historical documents making it a historical enigma for over two thousand years. The Warring States Period was an age of conflict among various states, during which the Zhongshan State developed its power gradually through struggles against other states such as the Yan, Zhao, Wei, and Qi. At the beginning of the Warring States Period, Zhongshan was conquered by a famous general, Yue Yang of Wei in 406 BC, but it regained its independence in 377 BC under the reign of Duke Huan who moved the capital of the state to Lingshou. The Zhongshan State reached the peak of its power during the reign of King Cuo of Zhongshan who proclaimed himself king and invaded the state of Yan occupying dozens of cities in the Yan State and demonstrating that Zhongshan had a power equal to any of the other leading states at that time. The descendants of King Cuo, however, proved less capable and increasingly extravagant, and this eventually led to the overthrow of Zhongshan by the Zhao in 296 BC.

Since the 1970s, archaeologists have been studying the ancient city of Lingshou, the capital of the Zhongshan State near present day Sanji village, Pingshan County, Hebei Province. They have excavated many tombs of nobles and civilians there and have uncovered nearly 20,000 artefacts. This excavation has begun to reveal the secrets of the mysterious Zhongshan State.

序言

::中山国是战国时期五个『千乘之国』之一,是仅次于『战国七雄』的诸侯国。中山国为游牧民族白狄鲜虞所建,历史短暂,史载缺略,遗迹湮没于地下,两千多年来鲜为人知,故称『神秘王国』。两千多年前,战国乱世,礼坏乐崩,诸侯雄起,中山国与燕、赵、魏、齐抗衡,几经沉浮。战国初,魏国势强,乐羊灭中山。后中山桓公复国,迁都灵寿,国力渐盛,至中山王䰀时,称王耀兵于太行山下,北略燕『方数百里,列城数十』,与七雄相比亦无逊色。然而物盛必衰,中山国外有强敌环伺,在内其统治阶层日益骄奢,国力渐衰。最终,在强大赵国的打击下走向灭亡。

::20世纪70年代以来,考古工作者在河北省平山县三汲村附近勘探了中山国都城灵寿古城,先后发掘了多座中山王族墓和平民墓。恢宏的王城遗址与近两万件出土器物,使这个『神秘王国』中山国逐渐向世人展现出其历史真容。

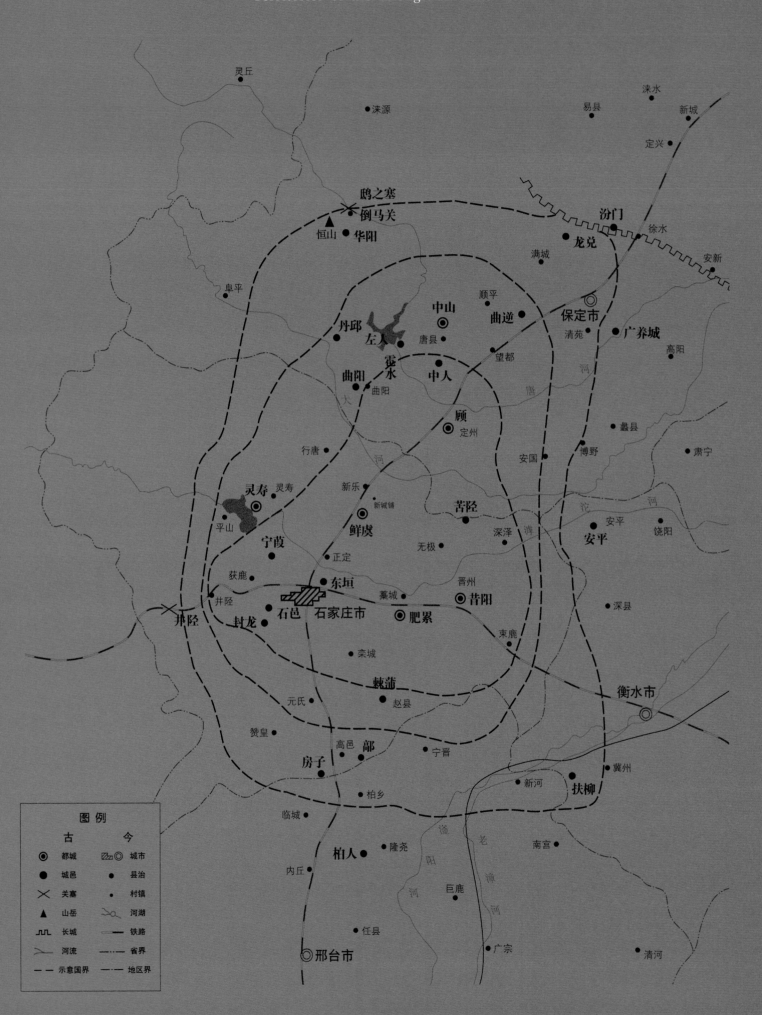

第一部分 鲜虞中山

:: 中山国是北方游牧民族白狄的一个部族鲜虞所建立的诸侯国。春秋时白狄的实力已颇为强盛，与秦晋关系密切，在两国或拉拢或打击下，白狄先后臣服于秦或晋。晋悼公时，迫于秦国压迫以及晋国和戎政策的诱惑，白狄东迁，他们从今陕西西北迁至山西盂县、昔阳一带，后来其中一个部落鲜虞继续迁徙，来到河北正定、新乐一带，并以此为根据地建立中山国，此后都城曾经三迁，最终建都于河北灵寿古城。

:: 中山国积极吸收中原文明，不断完善其礼乐制度，并保留游牧民族的风俗习惯，形成了独具特色的中山国文化。

First Part: Foundation of the Zhongshan State

The Zhongshan State was founded by Xianyu, a tribe from the northern nomadic ethnic group Baidi. The strong Baidi kept close relationships with the Qin and Jin during the Spring and Autumn Period, but later surrendered first to the Qin and then to the Jin state. During the reign of Duke Dao of Jin, the Baidi moved from northwest Shaanxi to a region in Yu County and Xiyang, Shanxi Province, to escape attacks by the Qin initially and was influenced by the annexation policies of the Jin. Later the Xianyu tribe of Baidi kept moving to the area that is now modern Zhengding and Xinle, Hebei Province, where the Zhongshan State was founded, and after several three other sites were made capitals for short periods, the capital of the state was finally permanently located at the ancient city of Lingshou.

The Zhongshan State absorbed the civilization of the Central Plains region. Using this, it incorporated the rituals of that civilization whilst retaining its systems as a nomadic people, thereby forming a unique state culture.

战国中山国地理位置示意图（公元前350年）

Location of the Zhongshan State (In 350 B.C.)

中山国君世系表
Kings of the Zhongshan State

中山国君	在位时间
文公	？——公元前415年
武公	约公元前414年——公元前407年
桓公	约公元前406年——公元前340年
成公	约公元前339年——公元前328年
王𰯼（cuò）	约公元前327年——公元前313年
王𡭗蚉（zǐ zī）	公元前312年——公元前296年
王尚	公元前296年——公元前295年

河北省平山县三汲乡中山国遗址

Panorama of the Site of the Zhongshan State in Sanji Town of Pingshan County, Hebei Province

金丝圈耳环

Gold earrings

Middle Spring and Autumn Period
Diameter 4cm | weight 6g (each)
Unearthed from the Tomb of Xianyu in Pingshan County,
Shijiazhuang City, Hebei Province
Collected by the Cultural Relics Institute of Hebei Province

∷ 春秋中期
∷ 直径4厘米 ∷ 每个重6克
∷ 河北省石家庄市平山县访驾庄鲜虞族墓出土
∷ 河北省文物研究所藏

◎ 用细金条盘成多环状，两头稍尖。出土时仍立于墓主人头骨两侧的耳根处。

嵌松石虎形金饰片

战国早期
每件长4.7厘米 :: 高1.8厘米 :: 重6.5~7克
河北省保定市唐县钓鱼台村出土
河北省文物研究所藏

为镶嵌在衣物上的饰件，具有浓郁的北方游牧民族特色。形象稚拙可爱。金黄的虎身上嵌有翠绿的松石，色彩明丽，富有极强的装饰效果。小虎低头垂尾，四肢弯曲作行走状。

A set of turquoise inlaid gold ornaments in tiger form

Early Warring States Period
Length 4.7cm | height 1.8cm | weight 6.5~7g
Unearthed from Diaoyutai Village, Tang County, Baoding City, Hebei Province
Collected by the Cultural Relics Institute of Hebei Province

Stone figures
Middle or Late Warring States Period
Height 7~8.4cm
Unearthed from the pottery workshop at Lingshou, Pingshan County, Shijiazhuang City, Hebei Province
Collected by the Cultural Relics Institute of Hebei Province

石板人形俑

∷ 战国中晚期
∷ 高7~8.4厘米
∷ 河北省石家庄市平山县灵寿古城陶器作坊遗址出土
∷ 河北省文物研究所藏

○ 共出土12件，仅3件完整。灰色片岩制成，人形，眉眼和口雕刻清晰，头顶中部束有发髻，可能属于「信圭」之类。

胡服俑铜器足

:: 战国中期
:: 高4.5厘米
:: 河北省石家庄市平山县中山王䰠墓出土
:: 河北省文物研究所藏

◎ 发现于中山王䰠墓墓前平台上。人俑头分发结小辫，面部饱满，眉骨和颧骨较高。双足并拢，蹲身，上身左扭，昂首挺胸，目光前视，左手压右腕，右手扶膝。上衣窄袖紧口，左衽衣，长及臀，系宽带，衣饰回纹。胸前有泡饰，左衽有钮结。腿、脚赤裸，肌肉丰满。服饰与汉服的宽袍广袖明显不同，应是当时的胡服。

Bronze leg of a vessel in the shape of a nomad figure
Middle Warring States Period
Height 4.5cm
Unearthed from the Tomb of King Cuo of the Zhongshan State, Pingshan County, Shijiazhuang City, Hebei Province
Collected by the Cultural Relics Institute of Hebei Province

铜孔雀饰

::战国中期
::长6.2厘米::高9厘米::身宽4.2厘米::羽宽6.5厘米
::河北省石家庄市灵寿县岗北村中山国墓群出土
::河北省文物研究所藏

◎ 出土1对2件，形制大小相同。孔雀铜铸，中空。孔雀直立于一铜板上，羽毛丰满，后尾高高翘起，似在开屏。此件与车构件一同出土，应该属于车上饰件。

Bronze peacock shaped ornaments from a chariot
Middle Warring States Period
Length 6.2cm | height 9cm | width 4.2cm | width of feather 6.5cm
Unearthed from the tombs of the Zhongshan State at Gangbei Village, Lingshou County, Shijiazhuang City, Hebei Province
Collected by the Cultural Relics Institute of Hebei Province

陶人俑拜山

:: 战国中晚期
:: 人俑高10.2厘米 :: 山形体高6~6.5厘米 :: 器底直径4.3厘米
:: 河北省石家庄市平山县灵寿古城铜铁器作坊遗址出土
:: 河北省文物研究所藏

◎ 这套组合由6件方锥体和1件人俑组成，均为泥质红陶。人俑直立，作拱手拜山状，线条简单粗犷，形态传神。人俑拜山发现于冶铜炉作业坑边的上龛，以净土掩埋，六个方锥体分为两组斜向排成两列，中间高、两侧低，组成『山』字形。人俑立于其后中间，形象地反映了中山国崇拜山神的风俗。

Pottery sculptures of a figure worshipping mountains

Middle or Late Warring States Period
Height of figurine 10.2cm ǀ height of mountains 6~6.5cm ǀ diameter of base 4.3cm
Unearthed from the bronze and iron workshop at Lingshou, Pingshan County, Shijiazhuang City, Hebei Province
Collected by the Cultural Relics Institute of Hebei Province

山形陶垫器

∷ 战国中期
∷ 高2~2.6厘米
∷ 河北省石家庄市平山县中山国王族5号墓出土
∷ 河北省文物研究所藏

◎ 器形为山锥体，底部平，顶部呈圆尖状，表面磨光无饰。此类器物在陶窑遗址内常有发现，属于烧陶器时的底垫。

Mountain shaped pottery paddles

Middle Warring States Period
Height 2~2.6cm
Unearthed from a Zhongshan noble's tomb No.5, Pingshan County,
Shijiazhuang City, Hebei Province
Collected by the Cultural Relics Institute of Hebei Province

中山山字形器

仪仗礼器。器物上部呈「山」字形，下部正中接圆筒状銎可安插木柱，其两侧内折成「透空雷纹」字纹。銎上端四口紧卡住「山」字的中锋，銎两侧有方形楔孔，出土时銎内残留朽木。銎的外侧下方刻有文字或符号。「山」字形器插在木柱上竖立排列，气势雄伟，象征中山王的权威，是中山国特有的青铜器。

圆形帐复原构想一

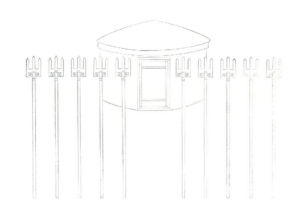

圆形帐复原构想二

山字形器

:: 战国中期
:: 高143厘米 :: 宽80厘米 :: 厚0.5厘米 :: 重44.6千克
:: 河北省石家庄市平山县中山成公墓出土
:: 河北省文物研究所藏

○ 共出土6件，出土于东西库内随葬器物之上。6件山字形器为同一铸模内浇铸成型后，经修正磨光后组装成一件整器。

Artefact shaped like the Chinese character *Shan*（山）
Middle Warring States Period
Height 143cm | width 80cm | thickness 0.5cm | weight 44.6kg
Unearthed from the Tomb of Duke Cheng of the Zhongshan State, Pingshan County, Shijiazhuang City, Hebei Province
Collected by the Cultural Relics Institute of Hebei Province

山字形器

Artefact shaped like the Chinese character *Shan*（山）
Middle Warring States Period
Height 119cm | width 74cm | thickness 1.2cm
Unearthed from the Tomb of King Cuo of the Zhongshan State, Pingshan County, Shijiazhuang City, Hebei Province
Collected by the Cultural Relics Institute of Hebei Province

∷ 战国中期
∷ 高119厘米∷宽74厘米∷厚1.2厘米
∷ 河北省石家庄市平山县中山王䯱墓二号车马坑出土
∷ 河北省文物研究所藏

◎ 共出土5件，出土于二号车马坑。器形成「山」字形。器上部出三支有刃锋体，两侧向下卷内成镂空雷纹状，下部中间有圆筒状銎，可插在立柱上，銎的前后两侧有方形楔孔。这种礼器为中山国所特有，造型庄重，立于木柱之上排列在帐前，象征着中山国国王的权威。

玉人与服饰

中山王族墓中出土了一些造型简洁的薄片玉人佩。小玉人为随葬人俑,有妇女、儿童形象。女俑头梳牛角形或圆形发髻,身着圆领窄袖束腰长袍,袍上饰有花格纹,是战国时期鲜虞人特有的发型和服饰,为研究战国时期少数民族服饰提供了重要的实物资料。

小玉人

::: 战国中期
::: 高2.5~4厘米
::: 河北省石家庄市平山县中山王族3号墓出土
::: 河北省文物研究所藏

Jade Figurines
Middle Warring States Period
Height 2.5~4cm
Unearthed from a Zhongshan noble's tomb No.3, Pingshan County, Shijiazhuang City, Hebei Province
Collected by the Cultural Relics Institute of Hebei Province

○ 中山王族3号墓共出土13件小玉人，其中5件残缺。小玉人用较好的白玉、墨玉、黄玉、青玉先锯成片状，再雕刻成人形，有男童和年轻女性及中年女性的形象。女性头梳牛角形双髻，身穿圆领窄袖对襟衫，下身穿方格长筒裙，双手在腹部用右手握住左手腕，圈手而立。年轻女性长发浓密，身材丰满，牛角形双髻也显得粗壮。中年女性头上的牛角形双髻显得较小。男童为单髻盘于头顶。

蟠螭纹兽首流嵌松石铜匜

:: 战国早期
:: 通长37厘米 :: 宽34.5厘米 :: 高34.2厘米
:: 河北省保定市唐县北城子村出土
:: 河北省文物研究所藏

◎ 匜是古代贵族的盥洗用具，与铜盘配套使用。盥洗时，用匜从上面浇水，下面用盘承接弃水。此匜器身椭圆，深腹，小平底，矮圈足。匜的流口为兽头状，兽耳挺立，双眼镶嵌绿松石，兽口张开形成流口，憨态可掬。兽身两侧饰铺首衔环，颈下有一环，尾部有一兽形鋬。匜的上腹铸两周凸绳纹，绳纹间为蟠螭图案，绳纹下作三角兽面纹，圈足外表作绹索纹。器身硕大，造型浑朴生动。

Bronze *Yi* pourer with a beast mask shaped spout
Early Warring States Period
Length 37cm | width 34.5cm | height 34.2cm
Unearthed from Beichengzi Village, Tang County, Baoding City, Hebei Province
Collected by the Cultural Relics Institute of Hebei Province

凤首流铜匜

::战国早期
::高16.5厘米∷口径11〜14.9厘米
::河北省保定市唐县北城子村出土
::河北省文物研究所藏

◎ 通体状若飞凤,流作凤首形,喙部可以启合,倒水时自动张开。匜身椭圆,大口斜沿,圆底,下有3个兽面纹蹄形高足,尾部有枭首蛇身环形鋬。腹部两侧各有一铺首衔环。凤首雕刻精致,尖喙、矮冠、圆目,眼圈饰羽毛纹一周,头部空白处阴刻流畅的云纹和鳞纹。铺首周围阴刻展开的凤翅,内底浅雕四条鱼纹。造型轻盈秀丽,花纹精细,是战国青铜器中的珍品。

Bronze *Yi* pourer with a phoenix head shaped spout
Early Warring States Period
Height 16.5cm | mouth diameter 11~14.9cm
Unearthed from Beichengzi Village, Tang County, Baoding City, Hebei Province
Collected by the Cultural Relics Institute of Hebei Province

双耳铜扁壶

战国中期
高33.1厘米 口径12.2厘米
河北省石家庄市平山县中山成公墓出土
河北省文物研究所藏

Double earred bronze *Hu* wine jar
Middle Warring States Period
Height 33.1cm | diameter of mouth 12.2cm
Unearthed from the Tomb of Duke Cheng of the Zhongshan State,
Pingshan County, Shijiazhuang City, Hebei Province
Collected by the Cultural Relics Institute of Hebei Province

◎ 共出土两件，大小相同，一件缺盖。出土于西库。器体呈扁长圆形，口外敞，短颈，溜肩，两环耳，鼓腹，平底，圈足。此壶模仿北方游牧民族马上所用盛水或酒的皮囊，三横一竖宽条纹仿佛皮带一样勒住扁壶。

络绳窃曲纹铜壶

::战国早期
::高29.7厘米
::河北省石家庄市平山县穆家庄出土
::河北省文物研究所藏

◎ 平口微侈,短颈,平底,圈足。肩部有对称的竖环耳,下腹前后各有一竖环耳。器身上多条直绹索纹相扣,结成环孔,孔内饰雷纹。壶身分为18个方格网区,内饰窃曲纹,带有浓厚的北方游牧民族的特点。

Bronze *Hu* wine jar with knotted rope and curved band patterns
Early Warring States Period
Height 29.7cm
Unearthed from Mujiazhuang Village, Pingshan County, Shijiazhuang City, Hebei Province
Collected by the Cultural Relics Institute of Hebei Province

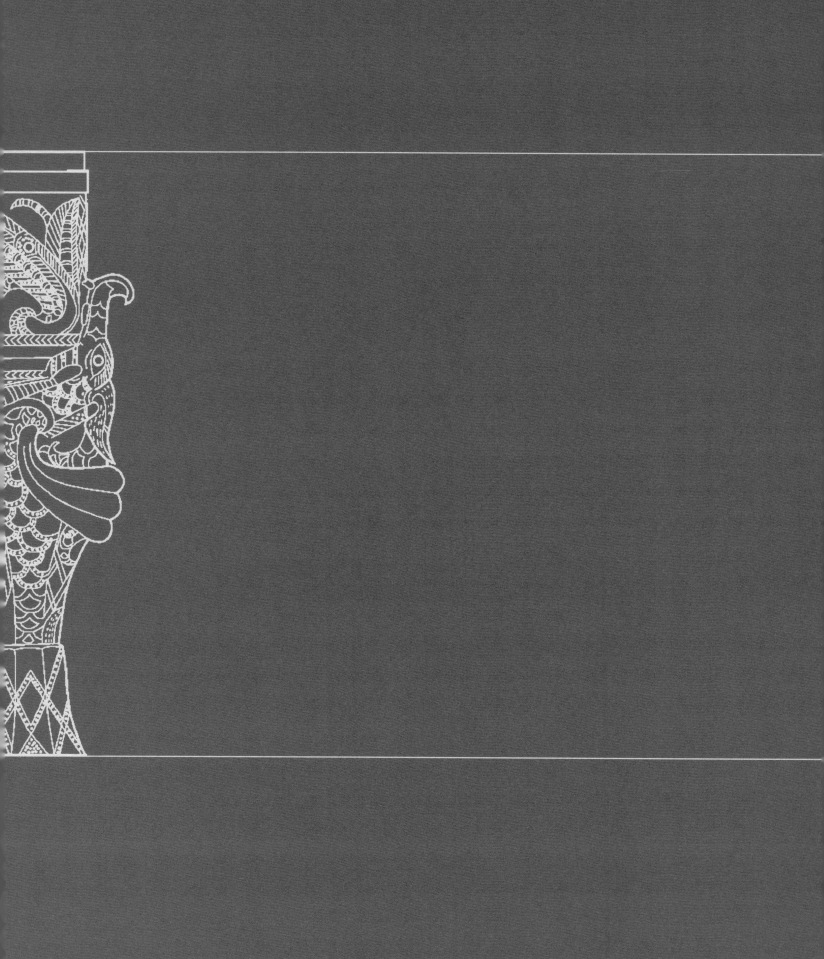

Second Part: Lingshou as the Capital

According to historical documents, the capital of the Zhongshan State was originally at Gu during the reign of Duke Wu and was moved to Lingshou during the reign of Duke Huan. Ancient Lingshou city, founded around 380BC, was located in present day Sanji, Pingshan County, Shijiazhuang City, in Hebei Province. The city was located with Taihang Mountain to the northwest, the Hutuo River to the south and the Jizhong Plain in the east. The city was divided into different functional areas: the palace area, the imperial burial grounds, a civilian residential area, a commercial area, and a workshop area. All the architectural components and exquisite artefacts unearthed from the palace ruins highlight a luxurious royal life in the Zhongshan State.

The governors of the Zhongshan State in Lingshou city included a total of five generations lasting 85 years: Duke Huan, Duke Cheng, King Cuo, King Zizi and King Shang. The state under the reigns of Duke Huan, Duke Cheng and King Cuo was relatively strong, when these pragmatic kings of the state advocated thriftiness, paying attention to political stability, integration of nationalities, and economic development. They also strengthened the military forces to expand the territory, so that the Zhongshan State developed rapidly and became "a state with 1,000 war chariots in its army", second only to the "Seven Leading Warring States".

第二部分 国都灵寿

∷ 史籍记载『中山武公居顾，桓公徙灵寿』。灵寿古城是中山国都城，位于今河北省石家庄市平山县三汲乡一带，约建于公元前380年。灵寿古城西北傍太行山，南依滹沱河，东临冀中大平原，地理位置优越。城内分为宫殿区、王陵区、平民居住区、商业区和手工业区，布局合理，功能齐备。宫殿遗址出土的建筑构件及精美文物无不彰显着战国中山王室生活的奢华。

∷ 都于灵寿古城的中山国君先后有桓公、成公、王䜣、王𧊒䘮、王尚，一共五代，历时85年。桓公、成公、王䜣时期中山国比较强盛，他们务实尚俭、励精图治、融合民族、勤修内政、发展经济、加强军备、扩充疆土，使得国势迅增，中山国成为仅次于『战国七雄』的『千乘之国』。

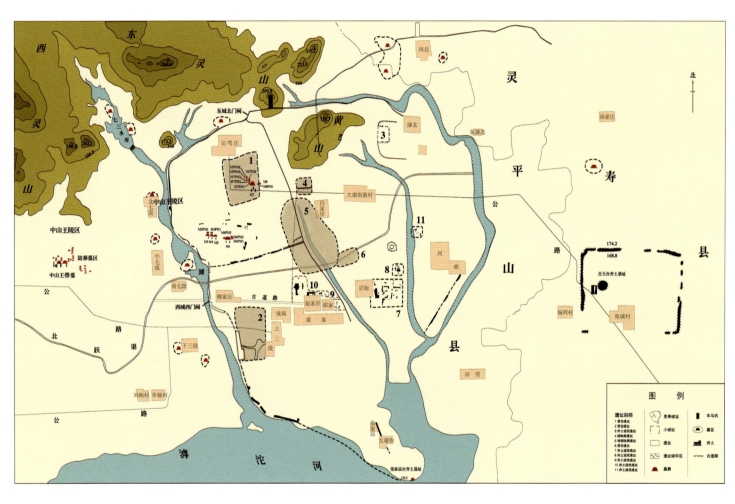

战国中山国灵寿古城遗址平面图

The Layout of the Capital City Lingshou and Royal Mausoleums of the Zhongshan State

灵寿古城

中山国后期的都城，位于今平山县三汲乡一带，约建于公元前380年中山桓公时期，作为中山国国都前后历时80余年。灵寿古城西北傍太行山，南依滹沱河，东临冀中大平原，地势形胜。古城依自然地形建成，平面呈桃形，南北长约4.5千米，东西宽约4千米。古城分为东城和西城，城内分为宫殿区、王陵区、平民居住区、商业区和手工业区，布局合理，功能齐备。中山国有"以山在邑中"的风俗，城内北部有小黄山，城内外分别有自然河沟自北向南流入滹沱河，既表示对山的崇敬，又可监督城内活动，在战争中还可起瞭望和指挥作用。东西城垣外分别有自然河沟自北向南流入滹沱河，成为天然的护城河。中山国长期受到燕、赵等国的军事威胁，在都城建设上高度设防，在城垣和城外的要害部位建有多处防御设施。簸箕掌，是灵寿古城东城的军事防御设施。在灵寿古城外东面的高坡上建有一个夯筑小城，城中最高点为军事设施"召王台"，具有监视、瞭望、报警及防御作用。

灵寿古城商业区一号房屋遗迹

灵寿古城宫殿区夯筑墙基

◎ 灵寿古城三号遗址内有大型夯土墙基及大量建筑构件，推测是中山国的宫殿遗址。

灵寿古城东城军事防御设施——镞箕掌

◎ 中山国长期受到燕、赵等国的军事威胁,在都城建设上高度设防,建有多处军事防御设施。

灵寿古城中心——小黄山

◎ 中山国有"以山在邑中"的风俗,既表示对山的崇敬,又可监督城内情况,在战争中还可起瞭望和指挥作用。

召王台

◎ 在灵寿古城外东面的高坡上,建有一个夯筑小城,城内修有高台,称"召王台",具有监视、瞭望、报警及防御作用。

灵寿古城城西护城河遗址

灵寿古城东城北垣

筒瓦·瓦当

灵寿古城的建筑构件中，筒瓦为半圆筒形。瓦当为筒瓦顶端的挡头，既能保护檐头，又有装饰作用。瓦钉是固定筒瓦的钉子。在中国目前发现的战国时期建筑构件中，山峰形瓦钉饰为中山国所独有。

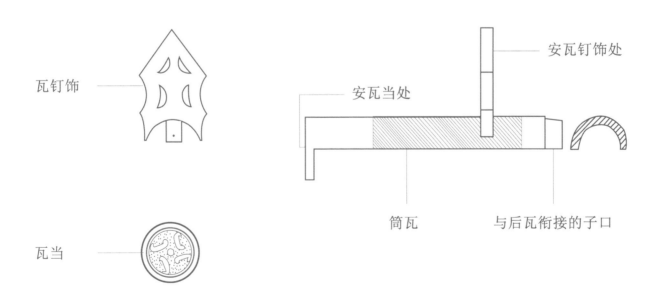

瓦钉饰

瓦当

安瓦钉饰处

安瓦当处

筒瓦

与后瓦衔接的子口

双鹰头山峰形瓦钉

战国中晚期
高37.2厘米∷宽27.26厘米∷厚2.4厘米
河北省石家庄市平山县灵寿古城陶器作坊遗址出土
河北省文物研究所藏

◎顶部为山峰，左右各饰一鹰头、曲颈、圆眼、勾状嘴。器身上部中间为三角形孔，下部为亚腰形和新月形孔，下端中部为扁方形瓦钉，无穿。下端左右出两翼，形似蝶翼，内侧呈半圆形，以便此饰件横跨于筒瓦上。在相接处均有用泥抹缝的痕迹。出土时器身全部涂朱，制作亦较为光滑精细。

Mountain shaped tile with nail decoration and a double eagle shaped head

Middle or Late Warring States Period
Height 37.2cm | width 27.26cm | thickness 2.4cm
Unearthed from the pottery workshop at Lingshou, Pingshan County, Shijiazhuang City, Hebei Province
Collected by the Cultural Relics Institute of Hebei Province

Clay flat tile

Middle or Late Warring States Period
Length 52.5cm | width 32~38cm | thickness 1.8cm
Unearthed from the bronze and iron workshop at Lingshou, Pingshan County, Shijiazhuang City, Hebei Province
Collected by the Cultural Relics Institute of Hebei Province

板瓦

∷战国中晚期
∷长52.5厘米∷头宽32厘米∷尾宽38厘米∷厚1.8厘米
∷河北省石家庄市平山县灵寿古城铜铁器作坊遗址出土
∷河北省文物研究所藏

筒瓦
∷ 战国中晚期
∷ 长51厘米
∷ 河北省石家庄市平山县灵寿古城宫殿建筑遗址出土
∷ 河北省文物研究所藏

Clay barrel tile
Middle or Late Warring States Period
Length 51cm
Unearthed from the site of palace in Lingshou, Pingshan County, Shijiazhuang City, Hebei Province
Collected by the Cultural Relics Institute of Hebei Province

乳钉双鹿纹半圆形瓦当

::战国中晚期
::长32.1厘米 ::宽19.3厘米
::河北省石家庄市平山县灵寿古城陶器作坊遗址出土
::河北省文物研究所藏

◎ 共出土8件瓦当，其中4件完整。当面饰有两只对称的母鹿，作回首状，四周饰有乳钉纹。瓦身饰细绳纹，后部顶端有一直径为1.5厘米的瓦钉孔，尾端处有子口式瓦唇。

Semi-circular eave tile with nipples and double deer patterns

Middle or Late Warring States Period
Length 32.1cm | width 19.3cm
Unearthed from the pottery workshop at Lingshou, Pingshan County, Shijiazhuang City, Hebei Province
Collected by the Cultural Relics Institute of Hebei Province

乳钉双虹云朵纹半圆形瓦当

:: 战国中晚期
:: 直径14.5厘米
:: 河北省石家庄市平山县灵寿古城陶器作坊遗址出土
:: 河北省文物研究所藏

◎ 共出土20件，仅1件完整，其余均残。当面饰有两道半圆形虹带纹，其间饰少量乳钉和冉冉上升的云朵。

Semi-circular eave tile with nipples, double rainbows and clouds patterns
Middle or Late Warring States Period
Diameter 14.5cm
Unearthed from the pottery workshop at Lingshou, Pingshan County, Shijiazhuang City, Hebei Province
Collected by the Cultural Relics Institute of Hebei Province

斗栱

斗栱是中国古代建筑特有的屋顶托架承重装置，直接承重的斗形方木称斗，架在斗上的弓形横木称栱。灵寿古城的建筑使用一些陶斗代替较小的木斗，至今不朽，是难得的战国实用斗栱遗物。

方形陶平盘斗

::战国中晚期
::长14.4厘米 ::宽13.7厘米 ::高7.2厘米
::河北省石家庄市平山县灵寿古城陶器作坊遗址出土
::河北省文物研究所藏

◎建筑构件。共出土5件，均为小型斗。5件陶斗分为平盘斗、交互斗和栌斗三种类型。

Clay building component
Middle or Late Warring States Period
Length 14.4cm | width 13.7cm | height 7.2cm
Unearthed from the pottery workshop at Lingshou, Pingshan County, Shijiazhuang City, Hebei Province
Collected by the Cultural Relics Institute of Hebei Province

长方形陶交互斗

::战国中晚期
::长15.6厘米::宽12.2厘米::高9.6厘米
::河北省石家庄市平山县灵寿古城铜铁器作坊遗址出土
::河北省文物研究所藏

Clay cross block building component
Middle or Late Warring States Period
Length15.6cm | width 12.2cm | height 9.6cm
Unearthed from the bronze and iron workshop at Lingshou, Pingshan County, Shijiazhuang City, Hebei Province
Collected by the Cultural Relics Institute of Hebei Province

成公升鼎一套

战国中期

- 通高46.0厘米 ∷ 口径41.8厘米 ∷ 腹径51.2厘米
- 通高33.3厘米 ∷ 口径32.8厘米 ∷ 腹径40.0厘米
- 通高32.8厘米
- 通高28.5厘米 ∷ 口径28.0厘米 ∷ 腹径31.4厘米
- 通高25.0厘米 ∷ 口径25.0厘米 ∷ 腹径29.5厘米
- 通高23.3厘米 ∷ 口径23.0厘米 ∷ 腹径26.5厘米
- 通高21.0厘米 ∷ 口径20.5厘米 ∷ 腹径23.8厘米
- 通高20.0厘米 ∷ 口径18.6厘米 ∷ 腹径21.0厘米
- 通高19.0厘米 ∷ 口径14.0厘米 ∷ 腹径17.2厘米

河北省石家庄市平山县中山成公墓出土

河北省文物研究所藏

◎ 出土于椁室西库西壁中部。升鼎用来盛放煮熟的肉食，是古代重要的礼器。西周礼制规定天子用九鼎，诸侯用七鼎。宴飨和祭祀时，九鼎中依次盛牛、羊、豕、鱼、腊、肠、肤、鲜鱼、鲜腊等肉食。战国时期礼坏乐崩，中山成公和王䶮死后都随葬了九鼎，反映出当时诸侯僭越礼制的局面，也体现了中山国国势的强盛。

A Group of bronze *Shengding* tripots belonging to Duke Cheng

Middle Warring States Period

Height 46.0cm | mouth diameter 41.8cm | belly diameter 51.2cm
Height 33.3cm | mouth diameter 32.8cm | belly diameter 40.0cm
Height 32.8cm
Height 28.5cm | mouth diameter 28.0cm | belly diameter 31.4cm
Height 25.0cm | mouth diameter 25.0cm | belly diameter 29.5cm
Height 23.3cm | mouth diameter 23.0cm | belly diameter 26.5cm
Height 21.0cm | mouth diameter 20.5cm | belly diameter 23.8cm
Height 20.0cm | mouth diameter 18.6cm | belly diameter 21.0cm
Height 19.0cm | mouth diameter 14.0cm | belly diameter 17.2cm

Unearthed from the Tomb of Duke Cheng of the Zhongshan State, Pingshan County, Shijiazhuang City, Hebei Province

Collected by the Cultural Relics Institute of Hebei Province

铜甗

战国中期

通高25.9厘米 ∷ 甑口径19.7厘米 ∷ 圈足径9厘米
∷ 釜口径7.6厘米 ∷ 腹径17.2厘米
∷ 河北省石家庄市平山县中山成公墓出土
∷ 河北省文物研究所藏

◎ 一大一小，出土于西库，此件为大者。甗，为古代蒸煮食物的炊具。由甑和鬲组成，上面的甑用来盛放食物，甑底为穿孔箅，下部的鬲用以烧水。此铜甗，甑敞口，折沿，方唇，圆腹，平底，圈足。腹部饰一道凸弦纹，两侧有一对兽面衔环。甑底箅孔为长条形，曲尺形。鬲的直领套接甑的圈足，圆肩，鼓腹，圜底，三足似鼎之蹄足，肩两侧有对称的铺首衔环，腹部饰凸弦纹一周。

Bronze *Yan* steamer

Middle Warring States Period
Full height 25.9cm | *Zeng* (upper) mouth diameter 19.7cm | bottom diameter 9cm
Fu (lower) mouth diameter 7.6cm | belly diameter 17.2cm
Unearthed from the Tomb of Duke Cheng of the Zhongshan State, Pingshan County, Shijiazhuang City, Hebei Province
Collected by the Cultural Relics Institute of Hebei Province

铜鬲

Bronze *Li* cauldron
Middle Warring States Period
Height 16.7cm | mouth diameter 15.6cm
Unearthed from the Tomb of King Cuo of the Zhongshan State,
Pingshan County, Shijiazhuang City, Hebei Province
Collected by the Cultural Relics Institute of Hebei Province

∷ 战国中期
∷ 高16.7厘米 ∷ 口径15.6厘米
∷ 河北省石家庄市平山县中山王䰩墓出土
∷ 河北省文物研究所藏

◎ 共出土4件，形制大小相同。出土于西库。带盖，盖顶圆鼓，盖面等距立3个云形钮。口微侈，口沿平厚，短颈，腹部微鼓，足中空。出土时器内有汤汁的结晶物。腹壁刻有铭文：「左使車（库）弧。」

铜平盘盖豆

Bronze *Dou* food vessel with a flat saucer
Middle Warring States Period
Height 24.6cm | diameter 19.5cm | weight 4.88kg
Unearthed from the Tomb of King Cuo of the Zhongshan State, Pingshan County, Shijiazhuang City, Hebei Province
Collected by the Cultural Relics Institute of Hebei Province

::战国中期
::高24.6厘米::直径19.5厘米::重4.88千克
::河北省石家庄市平山县中山王䰯墓出土
::河北省文物研究所藏

共出土1对2件,出土于东库。直壁,浅盘,平底,细长柄,喇叭形座。盖为平顶,顶面上有三钮。

铜方座盖豆

Bronze *Dou* food vessel on a square base
Middle Warring States Period
Height 26.3cm | length of base 14.4cm | diameter of mouth 13.4cm | maximum diameter 21cm
Unearthed from the Tomb of King Cuo of the Zhongshan State, Pingshan County, Shijiazhuang City, Hebei Province
Collected by the Cultural Relics Institute of Hebei Province

∷ 战国中期
∷ 高26.3厘米∷座长14.4厘米∷口径13.4厘米∷最大径21厘米
∷ 河北省石家庄市平山县中山王䰉墓出土
∷ 河北省文物研究所藏

◎ 共出2件，出土于西库。盖豆，造型敦厚。覆钵形盖，上有盘状捉手。豆身子口内敛，鼓腹，平底，束腰圆柄，高方座。口沿下两侧有一对环耳。方座一侧刻有铭文：「左使车（库），工弧。」出土时，器内壁附着食物痕迹。

Bronze *Fu* food vessel
Middle Warring States Period
Height 17.8cm | length 30.2cm | width 21.2cm
Unearthed from the Tomb of King Cuo of the Zhongshan State,
Pingshan County, Shijiazhuang City, Hebei Province
Collected by the Cultural Relics Institute of Hebei Province

铜簠

战国中期
高17.8厘米::长30.2厘米::宽21.2厘米
::河北省石家庄市平山县中山王䰯墓出土
::河北省文物研究所藏

○ 2对4件，出土于西库。簠为长方形，盖顶形盖，盖面四角各立一环钮。盖宽大，扣于器口。器身直壁，下部内折，平底，两端各有一环耳，底之四角各有一曲尺形足，足间有舌状或三角形饰。一足立面刻有："左使车（厙），工蔡。"出土时器内尚存干裂的食物。食物呈深褐色，颗粒较细，似为小米饭。4件铜簠盛放稻米饭和小米饭。

凤首提梁铜盉

::: 战国中期
::: 通高21.9厘米 ::: 口径10.1厘米 ::: 腹径22.4厘米 ::: 重3.7千克
::: 河北省石家庄市平山县中山王𰯼墓出土
::: 河北省文物研究所藏

Bronze handled *He* vessel with a phoenix head shaped spout
Middle Warring States Period
Full height 21.9cm | mouth diameter 10.1cm | belly diameter 22.4cm | weight 3.7kg
Unearthed from the Tomb of King Cuo of the Zhongshan State, Pingshan County, Shijiazhuang City, Hebei Province
Collected by the Cultural Relics Institute of Hebei Province

◎ 共出土3件，大小不一，出土于东库。铜盉是古代用于调酒、盛水的器物。铜盉的弓形提梁两端铸成龙头形象，龙吻连接两肩。提梁上套铜环，环的另一端接盖钮，以防盉盖脱落。盉流铸成凤首形，凤伸颈扬头，口部微张，似在婉转啼鸣，姿态矜持优美。弦纹下方自右至左横刻：「十一祀，右𠂤（使）车（库），啬夫郭痊，工㿝（触），冡（重）三百八刀。」弦纹上方刻：「右䇂者」，共二十字。

铜圆壶

::战国中期
::高43厘米 ::口径14.3厘米 ::腹径31厘米 ::重13.7千克
::河北省石家庄市平山县中山王䚇墓出土
::河北省文物研究所藏

Bronze *Hu* jar
Middle Warring States Period
Height 43cm | mouth diameter 14.3cm | belly diameter 31cm | weight 13.7kg
Unearthed from the Tomb of King Cuo of the Zhongshan State, Pingshan County, Shijiazhuang City, Hebei Province
Collected by the Cultural Relics Institute of Hebei Province

◎ 共出土10件，此器型为3对6件，出土于西库。带盖，侈口，平唇，有颈，溜肩，鼓腹，平底，圈足。盖顶微鼓，坡面有三个云头钮。肩部两侧各有一兽面衔环。出土时壶内有墨绿色酒液，香味浓郁。圈足立壁自右至左横刻：「左䈞（使）车（库）」，工弧。」

铜扁壶

::战国中期
::高45.9厘米 :: 宽36.5厘米 :: 厚15.3厘米 :: 口径15厘米
::河北省石家庄市平山县中山王䝮墓出土
::河北省文物研究所藏

◎ 共出土13件方壶、4件扁壶、10件圆壶。4件扁壶都出土于东库,此壶为一对2件。有盖、扁身、侈口、细颈、弧肩、圆腹、平底、长方形圈足。两侧肩部各有一兽面衔环。盖面微鼓,三个云头环钮。出土时,壶内有透明的浅翡翠色液体,经北京市发酵工业研究所化验鉴定为酒,是当时中国考古发掘中第一次发现的实物酒。

Bronze *Hu* flask

Middle Warring States Period
Height 45.9cm | width 36.5cm | thickness 15.3cm | mouth diameter 15cm
Unearthed from the Tomb of King Cuo of the Zhongshan State, Pingshan County, Shijiazhuang City, Hebei Province
Collected by the Cultural Relics Institute of Hebei Province

嵌勾连云纹铜方壶

::战国中期
::高45厘米 :: 口径11.3厘米 :: 腹径22厘米 :: 重6.3千克
::河北省石家庄市平山县中山王䰢墓出土
::河北省文物研究所藏

Bronze *Hu* wine jar inlaid with intertwined clouds pattern
Middle Warring States Period
Height 45cm | mouth diameter 11.3cm | belly diameter 22cm | weight 6.3kg
Unearthed from the Tomb of King Cuo of the Zhongshan State, Pingshan County, Shijiazhuang City, Hebei Province
Collected by the Cultural Relics Institute of Hebei Province

◎ 一对2件，出土于东库。方壶，器形周正，胎壁轻薄。四坡面各有一云头钮。直口，短颈，溜肩，鼓腹，平底，圈足。肩部两侧各有一兽面衔环。器身遍布勾连云纹图案，并镶嵌红铜、绿松石和蓝漆。壶体多种云纹相互缠绕，云气弥漫，五彩缤纷，雍容华贵，是战国青铜器中集多种装饰工艺于一体的代表作。每件器物于腹部一侧的下方横刻竖读：「十四祀，命冢宰䛑，所制省器作䛑者。」十六字，于器盖沿下刻同样阴文十六字，但多有漫漶。

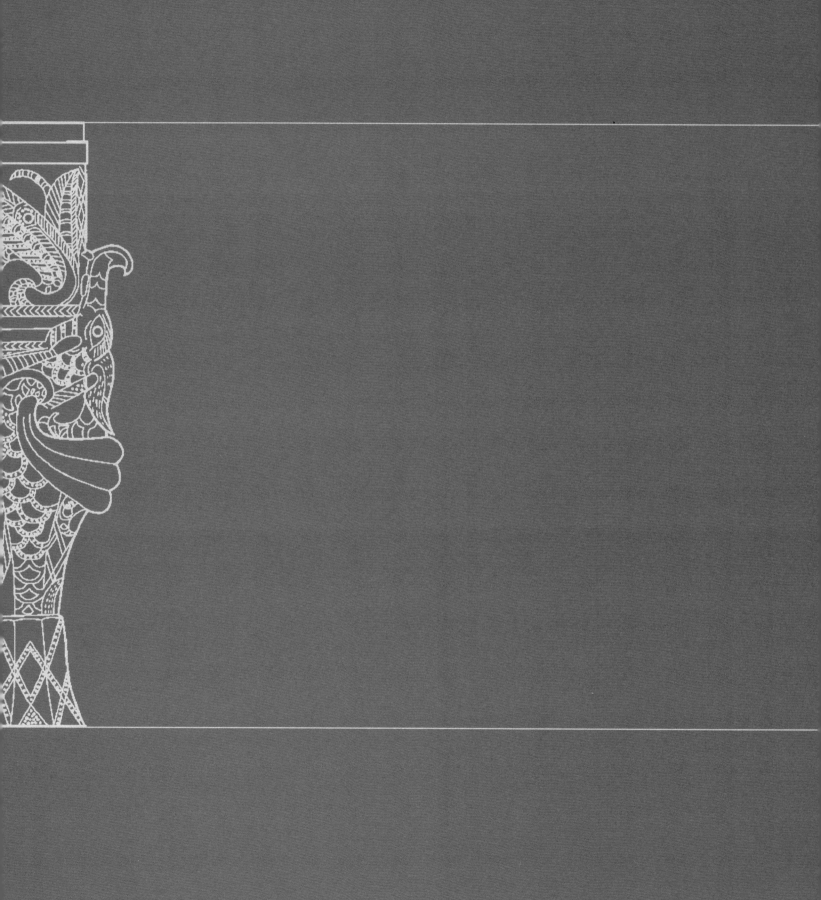

Third Part: Social Life of the State

Farming became the mainstay of the Zhongshan State, adopted as the primary mode of food production after it entered the Central Plains region. Productivity rose rapidly with the extensive use of iron tools in this period. The state was well placed to trade and had an excellent transportation network to Handan, the capital of the Zhao State to the south, the Yan State to the north, Linzi, the capital of the Qi State to the east, and the Dai State to the northwest. Many rivers in the state linked the Zhongshan State to the Qi State, and these promoted the development of a grain trade. Transportation and commerce contributed a lot to the development of the economy of the state, while pottery, wood, and silk industries also played important roles in its economy. The handicraft industry of the state was famous for the production of delicate artefacts and a wine industry also flourished. The advanced bronze and iron casting industry of the state showed not only a high level of technology, but was also one of great artistry and the artistic and romantic style of Zhongshan metalwork was the equal of the exquisite artefacts from the Chu State in the same period.

In the recent decades, a large number of extremely fine artefacts made of gold, silver, bronze, iron, pottery, lacquer, jade, and stone have been excavated from Zhongshan sites. They range from tools and everyday utensils to decorative objects and reflect all aspects of social life, including the politics, economy, and culture of a civilization that flourished over two thousand years ago.

第三部分 社会生活

进入中原地区后，中山国由游牧生产方式逐步转变为农耕生产方式，铁制农具的大量使用，推动了农业生产力的快速发展。中山国陆路交通南接赵国邯郸，北通燕涿，东到齐国临淄，西北可达代国。境内河流众多，水运可通齐国，粮食贸易规模发达。交通便利和商贸发达进一步推动了中山国经济的发展，制陶业、制木业、丝麻业等均为中山国经济的重要组成部分。手工业以"多美物"著称，酿酒业已有相当发展。铜器冶铸和铁器冶铸工艺先进，技术水平很高。北方各诸侯国中，中山国器物的艺术性和浪漫气息非常突出，与同时期奇幻诡异的楚国器物相比，也毫不逊色。二者一南一北，为当时的两朵奇葩，各有千秋。

近几十年，考古工作者发掘出土了大量精美的中山国文物，从材质上看有金、银、铜、铁、陶、漆、玉、石等，就使用功能上说有生产工具、生活和装饰用品，几乎涉及社会生活的方方面面，是两千多年前中山国政治、经济、文化的生动再现。

Bronze *Ben* adze
Middle Warring States Period
Length 10.6cm
Unearthed from a tomb at Gangbei village, Lingshou County,
Shijiazhuang City, Hebei Province
Collected by the Cultural Relics Institute of Hebei Province

铜锛
战国中期
长10.6厘米
河北省石家庄市灵寿县岗北村墓出土
河北省文物研究所藏

有肩铁铲
战国中晚期
残长14.8厘米
河北省石家庄市平山县灵寿古城铜铁器作坊遗址出土
河北省文物研究所藏

Iron spade
Middle or Late Warring States Period
Remained length 14.8cm
Unearthed from the pottery workshop at Lingshou, Pingshan County,
Shijiazhuang City, Hebei Province
Collected by the Cultural Relics Institute of Hebei Province

Pottery paddle with a round dot pattern
Middle or late Warring States Period
Diameter 11.6cm
Unearthed from the pottery workshop at Lingshou, Pingshan County,
Shijiazhuang City, Hebei Province
Collected by the Cultural Relics Institute of Hebei Province

圆点纹陶拍
战国中晚期
直径11.6厘米
河北省石家庄市平山县灵寿古城铜铁器作坊遗址出土
河北省文物研究所藏

铜斧 | 战国中期
:: 高7.6厘米
:: 河北省石家庄市平山县中山成公墓出土
:: 河北省文物研究所藏

Bronze axe
Middle Warring States Period
Height 7.6cm
Unearthed from the Tomb of Duke Cheng of the Zhongshan State, Pingshan County, Shijiazhuang City, Hebei Province
Collected by the Cultural Relics Institute of Hebei Province

Bronze *Zao* chisel

Middle Warring States Period
Length 19.9cm
Unearthed from the Tomb of Duke Cheng of the Zhongshan State, Pingshan County, Shijiazhuang City, Hebei Province
Collected by the Cultural Relics Institute of Hebei Province

铜凿
::战国中期
::长19.9厘米
::河北省石家庄市平山县中山成公墓出土
::河北省文物研究所藏

Clay Mold of a *Jue* pickaxe

Middle or Late Warring States Period
Length 16.5cm
Unearthed from the pottery workshop at Lingshou, Pingshan County,
Shijiazhuang City, Hebei Province
Collected by the Cultural Relics Institute of Hebei Province

陶钁范

::战国中晚期
::长16.5厘米
::河北省石家庄市平山县灵寿古城铜铁器作坊遗址出土
::河北省文物研究所藏

Clay mold of a knife
Middle or Late Warring States Period
Length 33cm
Unearthed from the pottery workshop at Lingshou, Pingshan County, Shijiazhuang City, Hebei Province
Collected by the Cultural Relics Institute of Hebei Province

陶刀范
::战国中晚期
::长33厘米
::河北省石家庄市平山县灵寿古城铜铁器作坊遗址出土
::河北省文物研究所藏

商业与货币是一对孪生兄弟。商品贸易发展到一定程度就会出现货币。早期中山国由于经济落后，不具备铸造货币的能力，主要使用晋国早期货币尖足布和燕国早期货币尖首刀。强盛时期的中山国，开始铸造自己的货币——成白刀币，并建立本国的货币流通体系。同时还流通邻国赵、燕的刀币和布币。这表明，战国时期各诸侯国之间的商业往来十分频繁。

银贝

::: 战国中期
::: 长3厘米 ::: 宽2厘米
::: 河北省石家庄市平山县中山王䰾墓北盗洞出土
::: 河北省文物研究所藏

◎ 仿天然海贝状，出土于椁室。正面圆鼓，背面平。中部纵开一口，错出齿状。模铸而成。据《礼记·丧大记》记载，棺饰有"齐，五采、五贝"，因此推断其为棺上饰物。

Silver shell currency

Middle Warring States Period
Length 3cm | width 2cm
Unearthed from a tomb (which had been previously holed in order to steal relics), north of the Tomb of King Cuo, Pingshan County, Shijiazhuang City, Hebei Province
Collected by the Cultural Relics Institute of Hebei Province

石贝

春秋中晚期
长2.9厘米
河北省石家庄市平山县访驾庄墓出土
河北省文物研究所藏

Stone shell currency

Middle or Late Spring and Autumn Period
Length 2.9cm
Unearthed from the tomb at Fangjiazhuang Village, Pingshan County, Shijiazhuang City, Hebei Province
Collected by the Cultural Relics Institute of Hebei Province

骨贝
战国中晚期
长2.8厘米
河北省石家庄市平山县灵寿古城商业区遗址出土
河北省文物研究所藏

Bone shell currency
Middle or Late Warring States Period
Length 2.8cm
Unearthed from the site of a commercial area in Lingshou, Pingshan County, Shijiazhuang City, Hebei Province
Collected by the Cultural Relics Institute of Hebei Province

磨背海贝

- 战国中期
- 长2.5厘米
- 河北省石家庄市平山县中山国王族4号墓出土
- 河北省文物研究所藏

◎ 中山王族4号墓在中山成公墓之西，属于王陵区内墓葬，有车马坑和一座陪葬墓。中山王陵墓葬方位制度：先王陵在北，子王陵在南，并向西偏移。兄弟之间的墓葬方位：兄长者位于东，弟位于西。因此，考古专家推测王族4号墓的主人应是中山成公的弟弟。

Polished shell currency
Middle Warring States Period
Length 2.5cm
Unearthed from a Zhongshan noble's tomb No.4,
Pingshan County, Shijiazhuang City, Hebei Province
Collected by the Cultural Relics Institute of Hebei Province

铜成白刀币

::战国中晚期
::长13.5厘米 ::宽1.5厘米
::河北省石家庄市平山县灵寿古城铜铁器作坊遗址出土
::河北省文物研究所藏

◎ 战国时期中山国自铸货币。首较钝,背稍弧,刃微凹。刀面廓线较凸,柄部有脊线,柄首环形。币面有「成旦(帛)」字样。

Bronze knife shaped currency inscribed with two Chinese characters *Cheng Bai* (成白)
Middle or Late Warring States Period
Length 13.5cm | width 1.5cm
Unearthed from the pottery workshop at Lingshou, Pingshan County, Shijiazhuang City, Hebei Province
Collected by the Cultural Relics Institute of Hebei Province

铜白化刀币

战国中晚期
长12.9厘米
河北省石家庄市平山县灵寿古城铜铁器作坊遗址出土
河北省文物研究所藏

◎ 赵国货币，钝首，刃略凹，背较直，也称"直刀"。柄上有两道脊线，柄首环状。币面有"白化"二字，"白"即"柏"，指"柏人"，地名，在今河北省隆尧县境内，战国时期属赵国。

Bronze knife shaped currency inscribed with two Chinese characters *Bai Hua* (白化)
Middle or Late Warring States Period
Length 12.9cm
Unearthed from the pottery workshop at Lingshou, Pingshan County, Shijiazhuang City, Hebei Province
Collected by the Cultural Relics Institute of Hebei Province

陶瓺

Pottery *Shuang* exfoliating tool for bathing
Middle Warring States Period
Length 27cm | width 6.7cm
Unearthed from the Tomb of Duke Cheng of the Zhongshan State,
Pingshan County, Shijiazhuang City, Hebei Province
Collected by the Cultural Relics Institute of Hebei Province

::战国中期
::长27厘米 ::宽6.7厘米
::河北省石家庄市平山县中山成公墓出土
::河北省文物研究所藏

出土于中山成公墓随葬大漆鉴（实为澡盆）中。长椭圆形，正面有戳印点组成的波折纹，点线细密，排列规整，图案精致，应为搓澡用具。《说文解字》有云："瓺，瑳垢瓦石。"

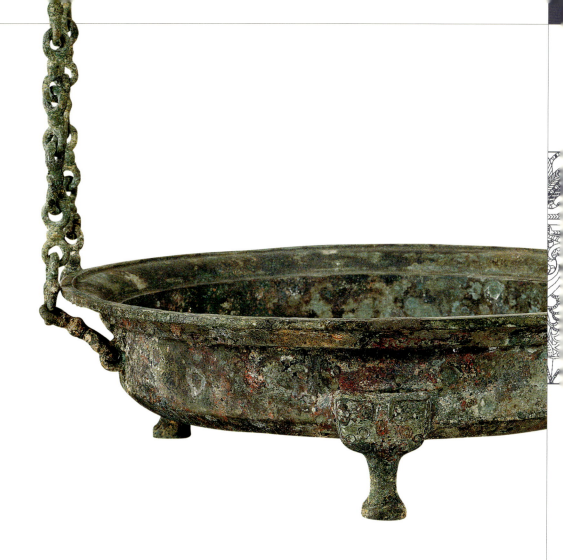

提链三足铜盆

:: 战国中期
:: 口径36厘米 :: 高10.1厘米
:: 河北省石家庄市平山县中山成公墓出土
:: 河北省文物研究所藏

共出土两件，形制相同，为取暖或烤肉用具。宽折沿，直腹，平底。三蹄足。盆两侧有环耳接提链，既可悬挂又可平置。提链由璜形龙首衔环提梁联结在一起。具有浓郁的中山国特色。

Bronze tripod heater with chain handles
Middle Warring States Period
Mouth diameter 36cm | height 10.1cm
Unearthed from the Tomb of Duke Cheng of the Zhongshan State, Pingshan County, Shijiazhuang City, Hebei Province
Collected by the Cultural Relics Institute of Hebei Province

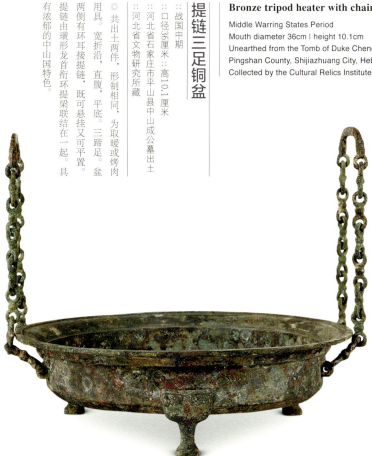

Bronze dustpan with handle
Middle Warring States Period
Full length 36.6cm | width 21.9cm
Unearthed from the Tomb of Duke Cheng of the Zhongshan State,
Pingshan County, Shijiazhuang City, Hebei Province
Collected by the Cultural Relics Institute of Hebei Province

有柄铜箕

:: 战国中期
:: 通长36.6厘米 :: 宽21.9厘米
:: 河北省石家庄市平山县中山成公墓出土
:: 河北省文物研究所藏

◎ 炭箕。平底，底面布满菱形或三角形镂孔，可以筛下木炭和碎渣，后端有八棱长柄，柄中有銎，可以安插木柄。

铜炭耙

Bronze charcoal rake
Middle Warring States Period
Full length 33.2cm | width 7cm
Unearthed from the Tomb of Duke Cheng of the Zhongshan State,
Pingshan County, Shijiazhuang City, Hebei Province
Collected by the Cultural Relics Institute of Hebei Province

:: 战国中期
:: 通长33.2厘米 :: 宽7厘米
:: 河北省石家庄市平山县中山成公墓出土
:: 河北省文物研究所藏

◎ 五齿耙，耙背镂饰卷云纹。中部铸一螭形兽，螭作向上攀爬状。前细后粗的圆管状长柄，柄端銎口再接木柄。炭耙与三足铜盆、有柄铜箕一同出土。

簋形铜灯

Bronze *Gui* lamp
Middle Warring States Period
Height 15.2cm | mouth diameter 18.2cm
Unearthed from the Tomb of Duke Cheng of the Zhongshan State,
Pingshan County, Shijiazhuang City, Hebei Province
Collected by the Cultural Relics Institute of Hebei Province

::战国中期
::高15.2厘米∷口径18.2厘米
::河北省石家庄市平山县中山成公墓出土
::河北省文物研究所藏

◎出土于西库。灯为扁圆形，圆腹，圜底，圈足。盖圆鼓，顶有支柱形钮，钮上有环。盖口一侧有合页连接簋身，使灯体与灯盖开合自如。点灯时翻开灯盖，支柱形钮支地，保持灯体稳定。闲置时，盖合起，簋身和盖紧密扣合。

勺

Bronze ladle
Middle Warring States Period
Full length 19.7cm | bowl of spoon 11.8 × 8.3cm | weight 0.38kg
Unearthed from the Tomb of King Cuo of the Zhongshan State,
Pingshan County, Shijiazhuang City, Hebei Province
Collected by the Cultural Relics Institute of Hebei Province

∷ 战国中期
∷ 通长19.7厘米 ∷ 勺碗长径11.8厘米 ∷ 短径8.3厘米 ∷ 重0.38千克
∷ 河北省石家庄市平山县中山王䰭墓出土
∷ 河北省文物研究所藏

◎ 共出土5件，形制大小基本相同，出土于西库。勺头为椭圆形，一侧接筒状直柄，筒内安黑漆木柄，出土时尚残存朽木，上下均有销钉孔，孔内尚有竹制销钉。柄背下部竖刻："左使（使）车（库），工䰭。"

云纹镂空铜匕

Bronze *Bi* spoon with hollowed out cloud pattern
Middle Warring States Period
Length 22.8cm | width 8.3cm
Unearthed from the Tomb of King Cuo of the Zhongshan State, Pingshan County, Shijiazhuang City, Hebei Province
Collected by the Cultural Relics Institute of Hebei Province

::战国中期
::长22.8厘米 ::宽8.3厘米
::河北省石家庄市平山县中山王䰠墓出土
::河北省文物研究所藏

◎ 匕为椭圆形，饰有四组卷云纹，直柄，有圆銎，銎内可插木柄。

镶金龙凤银带钩

:: 战国中期
:: 长18.6厘米
:: 河北省石家庄市平山县中山王䰿墓出土
:: 河北省文物研究所藏

◎ 琵琶形。钩头为螭首,钩身正面用金银交错镂雕出纠结在一起的蟠龙和凤鸟。金凤文静端庄,蟠龙生猛,回首张口,极富生趣。

Silver belt hook inlaid with a gold dragon and phoenix pattern
Middle Warring States Period
Length 18.6cm
Unearthed from the Tomb of King Cuo of the Zhongshan State, Pingshan County, Shijiazhuang City, Hebei Province
Collected by the Cultural Relics Institute of Hebei Province

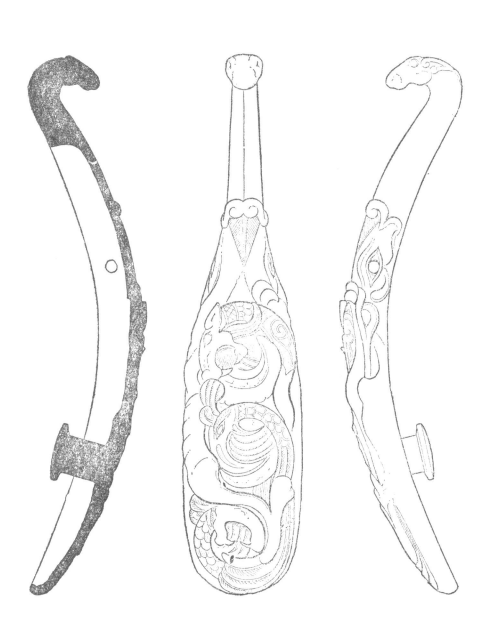

骨算筹

::: 战国中期
::: 长12.6厘米
::: 河北省石家庄市平山县中山成公陪葬墓出土
::: 河北省文物研究所藏

◎ 算筹是在算盘发明之前中国最重要的计算工具。中山国遗址出土的算筹有骨、玉两种。算筹的计数法遵循十进位制，以纵横两种排列方式来表示多位数目时，个位用纵式，十位用横式，百位用纵式，千位用横式，以此类推，遇零则置空。

Bone *Suanchou* counting rods

Middle Warring States Period
Length 12.6cm
Unearthed from an ancillary tomb attached to the Tomb of Duke Cheng of the Zhongshan State, Pingshan County, Shijiazhuang City, Hebei Province
Collected by the Cultural Relics Institute of Hebei Province

算筹用法示意图
Illustration of the *Suanchou* counting rods

石制六博棋盘

::战国中期
::长45厘米 ::宽40.2厘米 ::厚0.8厘米
::河北省石家庄市平山县中山王族3号墓出土
::河北省文物研究所藏

Stone *Liubo* chessboard

Middle Warring States Period
Length 45cm | width 40.2cm | thickness 0.8cm
Unearthed from a Zhongshan noble's tomb No.3, Pingshan County,
Shijiazhuang City, Hebei Province
Collected by the Cultural Relics Institute of Hebei Province

○ 中山王族3号墓在中山成公墓之西，属于王陵区内墓葬，有车马坑和一座陪葬墓。据考古专家推测王族3号墓的主人应是中山成公的弟弟。棋盘出土两副，大小相同，纹饰不同。六博，又称六簙、陆博，为古代棋类游戏。包括棋盘、棋子、箸、骰子。分黑、白两方，每方六子，一枭五散，故称六博，其中以枭为贵。双方先用骰子掷采，依掷采结果行棋，先杀枭者为胜。战国时期的游戏规则则已失传。

○ 中山国出土的两副六博棋盘，是目前发现年代最早的石质六博棋盘，系用青石板制成，盘面浮雕出饕餮、虎、蟠螭等纹样组成的图案。图案上下、左右两两对称，繁复而清晰。这两件棋盘将雕塑艺术和实用功能结合得完美无缺，是中山国能工巧匠的艺术杰作。

水晶棋子

::: 战国中期
::: 长2.4厘米
::: 河北省石家庄市平山县中山王族3号墓出土
::: 河北省文物研究所藏

◎ 共出土5颗，与石制六博棋盘相伴出土；水晶制成。一为长方柱体，使用痕迹明显。一为长方柱盝顶形，质地剔透，内有絮状物。

Crystal chess pieces
Middle Warring States Period
Length 2.4cm
Unearthed from a Zhongshan noble's tomb No.3, Pingshan County, Shijiazhuang City, Hebei Province
Collected by the Cultural Relics Institute of Hebei Province

铜独角兽壁插

战国中期
长5.4厘米
河北省石家庄市灵寿县岗北村中山国墓群出土
河北省文物研究所藏

Bronze unicorn shaped vessle stand
Middle Warring States Period
Length 5.4cm
Unearthed from the tombs at Gangbei village, Lingshou County, Shijiazhuang City, Hebei Province
Collected by the Cultural Relics Institute of Hebei Province

◎ 共出土2件。整体为半圆筒形，上面凸铸一伏地独角兽，作仰首状，翘尾。兽身饰卷云纹。在插端的两侧均伸出半圆形突起，器两端饰绚索纹。背面中间镂一长方孔。

玉玦

Jade *Jue* pendant
Middle Warring States Period
Diameter 5.9cm | edge width 1.4cm | thickness 0.3cm
Unearthed from the Tomb of King Cuo of the Zhongshan State,
Shijiazhuang City, Hebei Province
Collected by the Cultural Relics Institute of Hebei Province

战国中期
直径5.9厘米∷边宽1.4厘米∷厚0.3厘米
河北省石家庄市平山县中山王𰯼墓出土
河北省文物研究所藏

◎ 玦为有一缺口的环形玉饰，多用作耳饰或佩饰。呈双头龙形，龙身环状。上部正中部有一系孔。玦两面雕饰谷纹，有边棱。

谷纹黄玉璜

::: 战国中期
::: 长10.7厘米
::: 河北省石家庄市平山县中山王𰯼墓出土
::: 河北省文物研究所藏

○ 玉璜呈半环形，黄玉质，沁蚀处呈灰色。表面饰有谷纹，上中部有一系孔。

Jade *Huang* pendant with grain pattern
Middle Warring States Period
Length 10.7cm
Unearthed from the Tomb of King Cuo of the Zhongshan State, Pingshan County, Shijiazhuang City, Hebei Province
Collected by the Cultural Relics Institute of Hebei Province

墨书大理石片

Marble tablet bearing inked Chinese characters
Middle Warring States Period
Length 9.5cm
Unearthed from the Tomb of King Cuo of the Zhongshan State,
Pingshan County, Shijiazhuang City, Hebei Province
Collected by the Cultural Relics Institute of Hebei Province

∷ 战国中期
∷ 长9.5厘米
∷ 河北省石家庄市平山县中山王𰯼墓出土
∷ 河北省文物研究所藏

○ 大理石质。近三角形。其上墨书『壬申窆行與赵徣（桓）子匽吉』字样。

玛瑙环

战国中期
外径8厘米 :: 内径5.5厘米
外径4.2厘米 :: 内径2.7厘米
河北省石家庄市平山县中山王䰩墓出土
河北省文物研究所藏

◎ 此两件玛瑙环，大环半透明，内透淡黄色，环的内缘呈棱状，由内到外缘渐薄。小环呈乳白色，内外缘亦呈多棱状。

Agate rings

Middle Warring States Period
Outside diameter 4.2~8cm ǀ inside diameter 2.7~5.5cm
Unearthed from the Tomb of King Cuo of the Zhongshan State, Pingshan County, Shijiazhuang City, Hebei Province
Collected by the Cultural Relics Institute of Hebei Province

玛瑙串珠

:: 战国中期
:: 直径0.13~1.5厘米
:: 河北省石家庄市平山县中山王族3号墓出土
:: 河北省文物研究所藏

◎ 串珠共有222粒。玛瑙质，多为黄褐色，间以灰白、深蓝等色，颜色明润。

Necklace of agate beads
Middle Warring States Period
Diameter 0.13~1.5cm
Unearthed from a Zhongshan noble's tomb No.3, Pingshan County, Shijiazhuang City, Hebei Province
Collected by the Cultural Relics Institute of Hebei Province

Bronze fasteners inlaid with gold and silver patterns
Middle Warring States Period
Full length 10.7cm
Unearthed from the Tomb of King Cuo of the Zhongshan State,
Pingshan County, Shijiazhuang City, Hebei Province
Collected by the Cultural Relics Institute of Hebei Province

错金银铜四角接扣

- 战国中期
- 通长10.7厘米
- 河北省石家庄市平山县中山王䁐墓出土
- 河北省文物研究所藏

○ 共出4件，为方木框的四角相接处的铜构件。由一横一竖相垂直的两个部件组成。竖直部分整个透空，一边接木框，另一边有榫头插入横向部分一端的插孔内，并插栓固定。而横向部分另一端有銎口，接木框。两部分表面错金银蟠龙纹和凤纹。

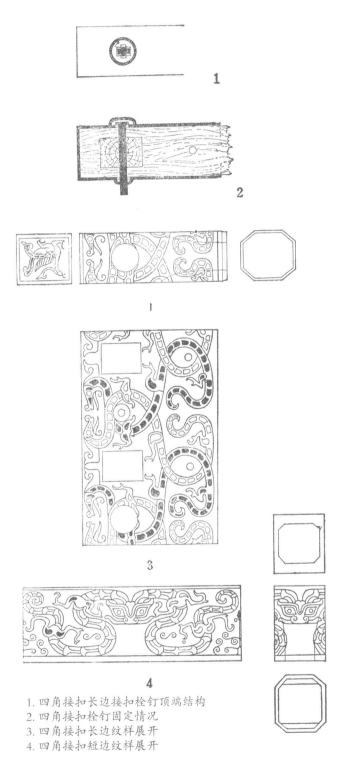

1. 四角接扣长边接扣栓钉顶端结构
2. 四角接扣栓钉固定情况
3. 四角接扣长边纹样展开
4. 四角接扣短边纹样展开

错金银铜四角接扣

长条形错银铜镶饰

战国中期
长77厘米 ｜ 宽6厘米
河北省石家庄市平山县中山王䱷墓出土
河北省文物研究所藏

Bronze ornaments inlaid with silver pattern
Middle Warring States Period
Length 77cm | width 6cm
Unearthed from the Tomb of King Cuo of the Zhongshan State,
Pingshan County, Shijiazhuang City, Hebei Province
Collected by the Cultural Relics Institute of Hebei Province

◎出土一对，长条板形，两端直折，直折外侧有半环形鼻。器身内侧两端有长方形横凸起，镶在木漆器上。器表满饰错银勾连云纹，繁复华丽。

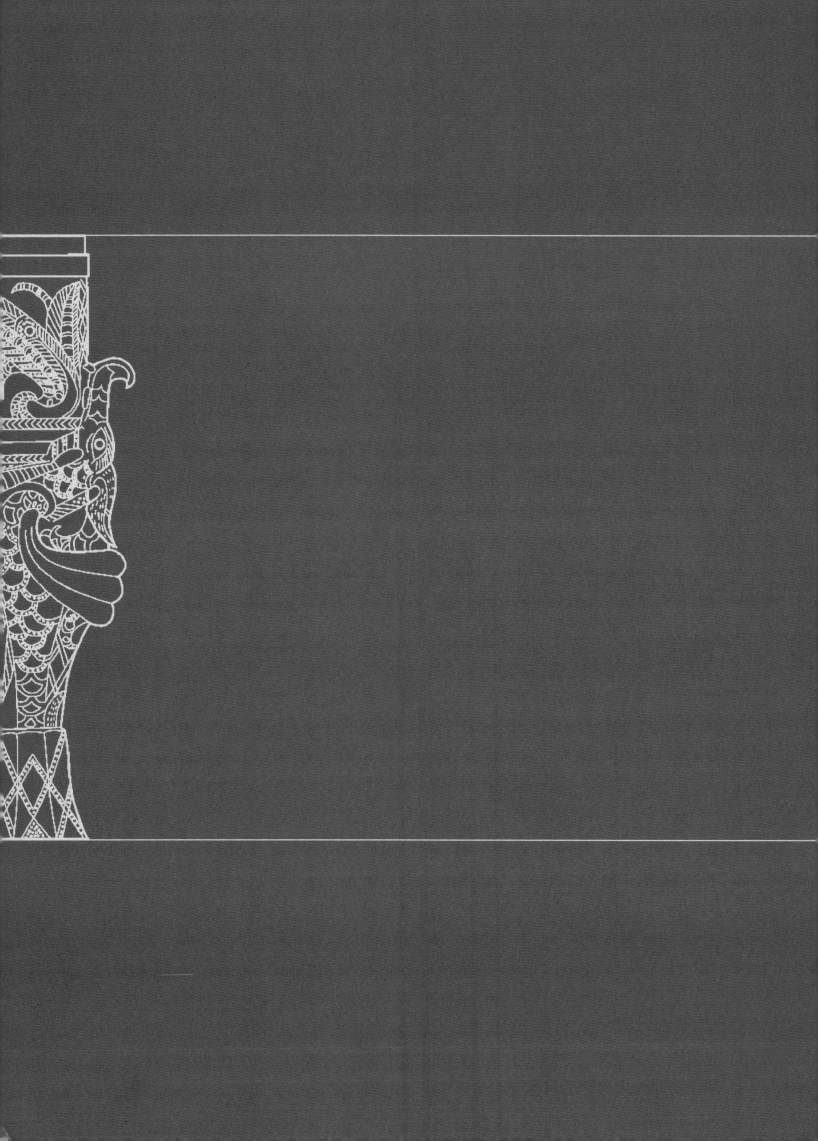

Four Part: Hunting and Military Affairs

The people of the Zhongshan State had a special interest in hunting and the martial arts, which doubtless lead to their proficiency in military affairs.

Hunting in the Spring and Autumn Period was not only an entertainment and a source of food, but also a type of military exercise. The Zhongshan people's nomadic history had fostered a passion for hunting and this sport lent itself easily to military matters. The Zhongshan army with its strong soldiers, sturdy horses, and excellent weapons fought continuously with the Jin in the late Spring and Autumn Period and with such leading states as the Wei, Qi, Yan and Zhao in the Warring States Period. Evidence of its military prowess is found in historical documents that record it defeated the two leading states of Zhao and Yan.

第四部分 田猎兵事

中山人喜猎、尚武、擅战。"萧萧马鸣，悠悠旆旌"——嘶叫的马鸣声，风中舞动的旌旗，好一派田猎的壮观景象。春秋战国时期的田猎活动既是娱乐，也是军事演练，带有游牧民族特色的中山国尤好田猎。中山国兵强马壮，武器装备精良，先后与春秋晚期的晋及战国时期的魏、齐、燕、赵等大国连续征战，《战国策·齐策》曾记：'中山悉起而迎燕赵，南战于长（房）子，败赵氏；北战于中山，克燕军，杀其将。'中山以千乘之国力而攻两个万乘之国，其国力之强可以想见。

中山国主要战事

公元前 530 年，晋荀吴率军借道鲜虞，进占昔阳（今河北晋县西）。

公元前 530 年，晋国灭鲜虞属国肥（在今河北藁城县境内）。

公元前 530 年，晋国攻伐鲜虞。次年，晋荀吴大败鲜虞，取中人城（今河北唐县西）。

公元前 527 年，晋荀吴克鲜虞属国鼓（今河北晋县境内），俘其国君鸢鞮（yuān dī）。

公元前 521 年，鼓国叛晋归鲜虞，晋国伐鲜虞。次年，荀吴灭鼓国，再俘其国君鸢鞮。

公元前 507 年，鲜虞在平中（今河北唐县西北）败晋军，擒晋国勇士观虎。

公元前 506 年，晋范鞅联卫伐鲜虞。

公元前 494 年，鲜虞与齐、鲁、卫共同伐晋，取棘蒲（今河北赵县境内）。

公元前 491 年，晋荀寅逃亡鲜虞。

公元前 489 年，晋赵鞅帅军伐鲜虞。

公元前 467 年，晋荀瑶智取中山属国仇繇（qiú yóu）（今山西盂县境内）。

公元前 467 年，晋荀瑶伐中山，取穷鱼（今河北易县或涞水县境内）之丘。

公元前 457 年，晋赵襄子派新稚穆子伐中山，占领左人（今河北唐县西北）、中人。

公元前 408 年，魏历三年占中山。

公元前 377 年，赵敬侯伐中山，战于房子（河北高邑县西）。

公元前 376 年，赵、燕伐中山，战于中人。中山败赵国，杀燕将。

公元前 332 年，齐、魏伐赵，中山国乘机决槐水围赵国鄗邑城（今河北高邑县东）。

公元前 314 年，燕内乱，齐攻入燕都，中山借机夺取燕国大片土地。

公元前 307 年，赵武灵王伐中山，到达房子。

公元前 306 年，赵武灵王伐中山，到达宁葭（今河北石家庄市西北）。

公元前 305 年，赵伐中山，攻取丹丘（今河北曲阳县西北）、华阳（今河北曲阳县恒山），鸱之塞（今河北唐县西北）。中山国献鄗、石邑、封龙、东垣四邑请和。

公元前 303 年，赵伐中山。

公元前 300 年，赵再伐中山，北至燕国、代郡（今河北蔚县一带），西至云中（今内蒙古包头市西）、九原（今内蒙古托克托东北）。

公元前 299 年，赵攻占中山。中山国君尚㙸逃亡齐国。

公元前 298 年，赵取扶柳（今河北冀县西北）及贯通中山国东西的滹沱河流域。

公元前 296 年，赵灭中山，迁中山王尚到肤施（今陕西榆林县东南）。

妾子䱷（zǐ zǐ）铜圆壶

战国中期

通高44.9厘米∷口径14.6厘米∷腹径31.2厘米∷重13.65千克

河北省石家庄市平山县中山王䗍墓出土

河北省文物研究所藏

Bronze *Hu* jar belonging to King *Zizi*

Middle Warring States Period

Full height 44.9cm | mouth diameter 14.6cm | belly diameter 31.2cm
weight 13.65kg

Unearthed from the Tomb of King Cuo of the Zhongshan State, Pingshan County, Shijiazhuang City, Hebei Province

Collected by the Cultural Relics Institute of Hebei Province

◎ 出土于东库。侈口平唇，短颈鼓腹，平底圈足。盖顶鼓，坡面有3个云形钮。肩部两侧各一兽面衔环，腹部两道凸弦纹。壶出土时盛满清水。圈足上刻有23字铭文，记壶的重量和制壶匠的名字。腹部刻有182字，是中山国君王妾子䱷为父亲王䗍写的悼词。悼词歌颂了先王的慈爱贤明，赞扬了中山国相邦司马赒率军攻伐燕国所取得的战果，具有重要的史料价值。

拓片 1

诸马逢子道逢或惟
战赐燕不道得不
怒诉亡义上贤辜
主惟子佐
辟司之司
臣其大马
反任辟赐
臣之（而
其邦辟家
（重）

拓片 2

罚厥无夕每者胤
以民疆不者扬嗣
忧之日忘先告盄
夜大王：盗
去慈昔敢
刑爱明
百

拓片 3

祗不孙功先以世永敬不
丞敬孙烈王追世祠命敢
祀寅子之庸毋新新宁
祗子 替地地处

拓片 4

潸可先呼隐德鲜以四驭
潸复王！逸行镐取牡右
流得之先先盛、鲜彭和
涕，德王王皇粮镐彭同
弗、，，祀、，，

拓片 5

会新猎朕里方大率不
如土、先，数启师能
林，苗王惟百邦征宁
。其夭，邦里宇燕处
彼田惟之，，，

拓片及释文：

◎ 盄盗圆壶铭文释意：（共计182字，重文5个）

◎ 拓片1：惟不辜，或得贤佐司马赒，而任之邦。逢燕无道易上，子之大僻（辟）不义，反臣其主。惟司马赒诉诤战怒

◎ 拓片2：胤嗣盄盗，敢明扬告：昔者先王慈爱百敏，笃胄无疆，日夜不忘，大去刑罚，以忧厥民之。

◎ 拓片3：不敢宁处，敬命新地，永祠先王，世世毋替，以追庸先王之功烈，子子孙孙，毋有不敬，寅祗承祀。

◎ 拓片4：驭右和同，四牡彭彭，以取鲜镐，粮祀先王，德行盛皇，悁像先王。呜呼！先王之德，弗可复得，潸潸流涕。

◎ 拓片5：不能宁处，率师征燕，大启邦宇，方数百里，惟邦之干。惟朕先王，苗夭田猎，于彼新土，其会如林。

狩猎宴乐图铜盖豆

Bronze Dou container with hunting and banquet patterns
Early Warring States Period
Height 19.6cm | mouth diameter 17cm | base diameter 10.4cm
Unearthed from the tomb at Mujiazhuang Village, Pingshan County, Pingshan County, Shijiazhuang City, Hebei Province
Collected by the Cultural Relics Institute of Hebei Province

::战国早期
::高19.6厘米 ::口径17厘米 ::底座直径10.4厘米
::河北省石家庄市平山县穆家庄墓出土
::河北省文物研究所藏

◎子母口，顶为圆提手，深腹，喇叭形圆座，豆柄为实心，器腹上部有两个对称的环状竖耳。全器通身均有凸铸纹饰，两环耳上饰花叶带纹，器盖捉手和器身上部饰狩猎、宴乐、采桑等图纹。

◎器盖上是两组相同的狩猎宴乐图：宴乐似在一座大堂屋中举行，屋顶为斜坡顶。二层楼台上堂内中间几条上放置2个壶，有6位贵族或持觚、或对饮。楼下的横梁上悬挂着4个编钟，4个编磬，皆从大到小，由左至右排列，周围有乐伎9人，均头梳牛角髻，身穿长衣裙，有吹笛的、有敲钟的、有击鼓的、有摇鼓的、有伴舞的等等。楼外为猎雁图：有人射雁，大雁或飞翔、或中箭跌落。豆腹部为狩猎图：有人持刀剑刺兽，有人操矛追逐等。

◎铜豆腹部铸有两组相同图案的狩猎图：每组图中有猎人14个，大多数为半裸体男性，他们手持长矛、戈、短剑、棍棒、弓箭等武器，正在与野兽肉搏。豆柄座上是两组相同的采桑和狩猎图。豆盖捉手上有一组狩猎图。整器共计有90个人物，63只野兽，26只鸟和6条鱼，纹饰繁密，形象鲜活，动感十足，气氛热烈。

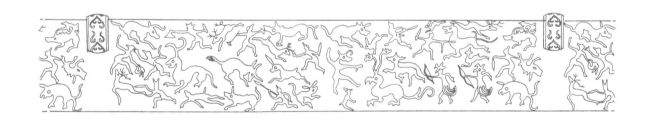

铜套盘

::战国中期
::口径18.35～20.4厘米 ::高3.55～3.7厘米
::底径10.9～14.2厘米 ::厚0.1厘米
::河北省石家庄市平山县中山成公墓出土
::河北省文物研究所藏

◎ 共出土2套10件，出土于西库。口微敛，浅腹，平底，胎极薄。素面。五个铜盘大小套叠，严丝合缝，多为出行时用，携带方便。

A set of bronze dishes
Middle Warring States Period
Mouth diameter 18.35~20.4cm
height 3.55~3.7cm
base diameter 10.9~14.2cm
thickness 0.1cm
Unearthed from the Tomb of Duke Cheng of the Zhongshan State,
Pingshan County, Shijiazhuang City, Hebei Province
Collected by the Cultural Relics Institute of Hebei Province

Bronze cover on the central post of the hunting tent
Middle Warring States Period
Height 29.2cm | diameter 39.5cm
Unearthed from the Tomb of King Cuo of the Zhongshan State,
Pingshan County, Shijiazhuang City, Hebei Province
Collected by the Cultural Relics Institute of Hebei Province

圆形猎帐柱顶帽

::战国中期
::高29.2厘米 ::直径39.5厘米
::河北省石家庄市平山县中山王䝨墓出土
::河北省文物研究所藏

柱顶帽呈蘑菇状，帽体为圆筒形，有錾。鼓顶，顶面有3个等距的三角形孔。直壁，壁的周圈等距分布15个半圆形环，环中各套一"凸"字形环，环边有鸭首状卡头。圆形军帐柱顶帽架设十分简单，即将柱帽安装在高柱之上，用十五条一端绾结成环形扣的绳索从帐帽吊环上面套入鸭首，然后呈辐射状拉向周围固定即可。中心帽柱与车和猎狗一同出土，应为狩猎时设帐所用。

屏风构件一组

Bronze hinge with a ring
Middle Warring States Period
Length 6.5cm | width 4.2cm | weight 0.23kg
Unearthed from the Tomb of King Cuo of the Zhongshan State,
Pingshan County, Shijiazhuang City, Hebei Province
Collected by the Cultural Relics Institute of Hebei Province

铜合页（带环）
::战国中期
::长6.5厘米 ::宽4.2厘米 ::重0.23千克
::河北省石家庄市平山县中山王譽墓出土
::河北省文物研究所藏

◎ 合页应安装于两屏扇后立框之上，使两个屏扇既联结又能张合，起着枢纽作用。合页的两页作长柱状，各有方孔可穿木钉，工艺十分精细。

Bronze hinges
Middle Warring States Period
Length 5.3cm | width 3.6cm
Unearthed from the Tomb of King Cuo of the Zhongshan State,
Pingshan County, Shijiazhuang City, Hebei Province
Collected by the Cultural Relics Institute of Hebei Province

铜合页
::战国中期
::长5.3厘米 ::宽3.6厘米
::河北省石家庄市平山县中山王譽墓出土
::河北省文物研究所藏

◎ 此类合页镶于屏扇之上框与折沿板之间，转轴后部为半圆形，可使合页的开合角度限定在180度之内。

Bronze hinge axis hooks
Middle Warring States Period
Length 15cm | width 1.4cm | weight 0.15kg
Unearthed from the Tomb of King Cuo of the Zhongshan State,
Pingshan County, Shijiazhuang City, Hebei Province
Collected by the Cultural Relics Institute of Hebei Province

铜活轴挂钩
::战国中期
::长15厘米 ::宽1.4厘米 ::重0.15千克
::河北省石家庄市平山县中山王譽墓出土
::河北省文物研究所藏

◎ 共出土二件。出土时位于上框两端合页之内，镶于两屏扇折沿板旁，为折沿时钩挂上框起加固作用。分为榫头、转轴、钩杆、钩头四部分。榫头长方形上有方形木钉孔，转轴圆形，可转动180度，钩杆长而直，内侧平，上面抹角，钩头方形，内侧平。

折叠式方形小帐构件一组

Bronze movable tube of a tent

Middle Warring States Period
Length 11.6cm | width 9.2cm | weight 0.8kg
Unearthed from the Tomb of King Cuo of the Zhongshan State, Pingshan County, Shijiazhuang City, Hebei Province
Collected by the Cultural Relics Institute of Hebei Province

活动铜接管

战国中期
长11.6厘米∷宽9.2厘米∷重0.8千克
河北省石家庄市平山县中山王䰽墓出土
河北省文物研究所藏

共出土4件，位于帐架的四个上角。其中DK:45-2上竖刻「十四祀」，左使车啟（造）。」七字，共二行。

Bronze crisscross poles of a tent

Middle Warring States Period
Length 30.2cm | diameter of pole 4cm | weight 3.14kg
Unearthed from the Tomb of King Cuo of the Zhongshan State, Pingshan County, Shijiazhuang City, Hebei Province
Collected by the Cultural Relics Institute of Hebei Province

十字形帐顶铜插管

战国中期
长30.2厘米∷管径4厘米∷重3.14千克
河北省石家庄市平山县中山王䰽墓出土
河北省文物研究所藏

Bronze *Jue* pickaxe

Middle Warring States Period
Unearthed from the Tomb of King Cuo of the Zhongshan State, Pingshan County, Shijiazhuang City, Hebei Province
Collected by the Cultural Relics Institute of Hebei Province

铜镢

战国中期
河北省石家庄市灵寿县中山王䰽墓出土
河北省文物研究所藏

铜镢上刻铭文：「十四祀，牀麀（cóng yáo），啬夫徐戬（zhì）剕（制）之。」

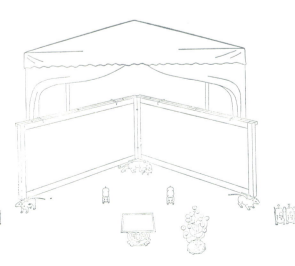

小帐及屏风复原示意图

◎ 小帐铜构件由一件帐顶十字形活动插管、四件活动接管和四个铜镢组成。帐顶铜插管为相互垂直的四段插管呈"十"字形连成。十字形插管连接四根帐顶杆，顶杆另一端连接活动铜接管的一头，铜接管的另一头接立杆。立杆插入铜镢侧面的两个环中，铜镢固定于地下。再蒙上帐布，即完成小帐的搭建。

◎ 出土时连接着帐杆的朽灰，束成一捆，似由帐顶部中心十字形活动插管和转角处活动接管连接着八根帐杆。帐杆为圆木，表涂黑漆，管外部分每根长1.69米。

◎ 屏风铜构件，有合页、活轴挂钩、卯眼套件、铺首、吊环、圆孔方形饰片、活轴拉手等。

错金银铜犀屏座

Bronze rhinoceros shaped screen stand inlaid with gold and silver patterns
Middle Warring States Period
Length 55.5cm | height 22cm | weight 19.35kg
Unearthed from the Tomb of King Cuo of the Zhongshan State, Pingshan County, Shijiazhuang City, Hebei Province
Collected by the Cultural Relics Institute of Hebei Province

::战国中期
::长55.5厘米::高22厘米::重19.35千克
::河北省石家庄市平山县中山王䰖墓出土
::河北省文物研究所藏

出土于东库。原两扇屏风由错金银虎噬鹿屏座、错金银犀屏座、错金银牛屏座支撑。犀，身躯肥硕，两耳侧立，双眼圆睁，长尾挺直，四肢粗壮，昂首挺立。头顶、额、鼻各有一角。全身用金、银宽双线错出黄白相间的卷云纹，简约而华丽。犀牛背上有銎口，用来插屏风的木榫。

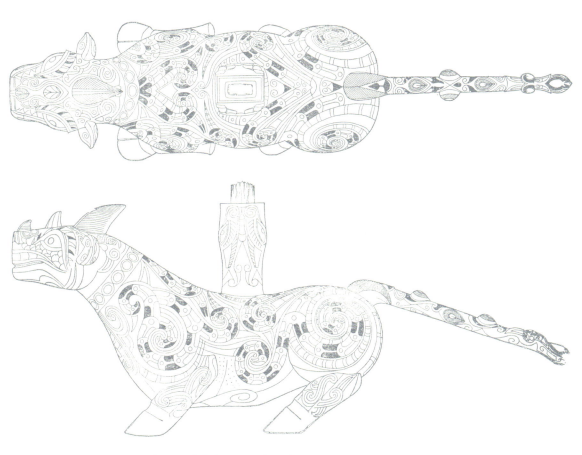

错金银铜犀屏座侧视、俯视图

错金银虎噬鹿铜屏风座

:: 战国中期
:: 通长51厘米 :: 高21.9厘米 :: 重26.6千克
:: 河北省石家庄市平山县中山王䶮墓出土
:: 河北省文物研究所藏

Bronze screen stand in the form of a tiger devouring a deer
Middle Warring States Period
Length 51cm | height 21.9cm | weight 26.6kg
Unearthed from the Tomb of King Cuo of the Zhongshan State, Pingshan County, Shijiazhuang City, Hebei Province
Collected by the Cultural Relics Institute of Hebei Province

◎ 为联结两扇屏风的中间插座，造型为猛虎噬鹿。猛虎身躯矫健，硬尾长甩，躬身右屈，正贪婪地将一只小鹿吞入口中，小鹿在虎口中无力地挣扎，勾勒出一幅大自然中弱肉强食的生动画面。老虎的后肢用力蹬地，前肢下踞，整个身躯呈弧形，虎的右前爪因抓鹿而悬空，借用鹿腿的支撑保持平衡，构思巧妙。通体错出斑斓的金片和银丝卷云纹，工艺手法为先设计好的花纹刻出沟槽，再将金片、银丝嵌入槽中，最后错磨光滑。虎的颈部和臀部有两个以山羊面装饰的长方形銎口，用来插放屏风扇。虎腹下有铭文："十四祀，牀麀嗇夫徐戠，制（制）省（省）器。"

错金银铜牛屏风座

战国中期
通长53厘米∷高22厘米
河北省石家庄市平山县中山王𰯼墓出土
河北省文物研究所藏

屏风插座之一。铜牛浑圆壮硕，尾巴挺直，四肢粗短有力。双目圆睁，两耳侧立，两角后倾，口部微张前伸，憨厚可爱。周身饰有错金银卷云纹，艳丽醒目。尾巴和尾根两侧用银线和金点错成鳞片纹，尾梢作长毛纹。牛背上有以山羊头面装饰的銎口，用来插放屏风扇，出土时銎内残存有木榫遗迹。器腹下有铭文："十四祀，牂䍧啬夫徐戠，𠣪（制）省器。"

Bronze bovine shaped screen stand inlaid with gold and silver patterns
Middle Warring States Period
Length 53cm | height 22cm
Unearthed from the Tomb of King Cuo of the Zhongshan State, Pingshan County, Shijiazhuang City, Hebei Province
Collected by the Cultural Relics Institute of Hebei Province

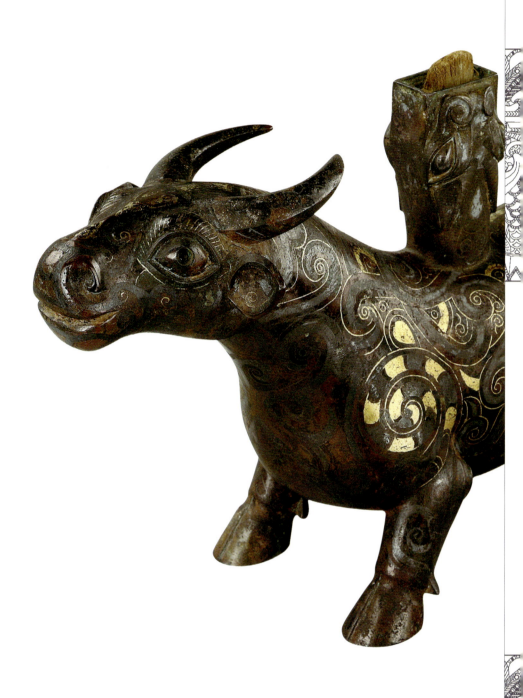

金银狗项圈

Gold and silver dog collar
Middle Warring States Period
Diameter 18cm
Unearthed from the Tomb of King Cuo of the Zhongshan State, Pingshan County, Shijiazhuang City, Hebei Province
Collected by the Cultural Relics Institute of Hebei Province

::战国中期
::直径18厘米
::河北省石家庄市平山县中山王䜣墓杂殉坑出土
::河北省文物研究所藏

◎ 共出土2件。出土于杂殉坑两具狗骨架的颈部。中山国盛行田猎，所养猎狗十分著名。随葬的两具狗颈上均戴金银项圈。项圈用长方形金片、银片卷成扁管状，相间连缀穿在革带上制成项圈。项圈上缀一铜环，用来结带。一件项圈由9枚金管和9枚银管穿成，银管共重63.3克，金管共重109.2克。一件项圈由各8枚金管和8枚银管穿成，银管共重65.1克，金管共重93克。为爱犬佩戴金银项圈，反映了中山国国王生活的奢侈。

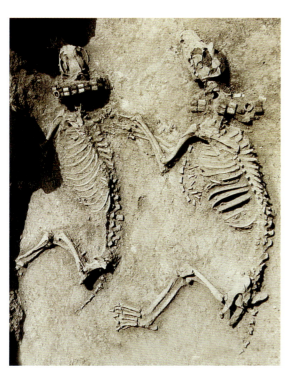

中山王嚳墓杂殉坑出土狗骨架

连贝纹铜环

战国中期
直径7.2厘米
河北省石家庄市平山县中山王䑞墓出土
河北省文物研究所藏

Bronze rings with a shell pattern
Middle Warring States Period
Diameter 7cm
Unearthed from the Tomb of King Cuo of the Zhongshan State,
Pingshan County, Shijiazhuang City, Hebei Province
Collected by the Cultural Relics Institute of Hebei Province

Bronze double rings with a round dot pattern
Middle Warring States Period
Length 7.2cm
Unearthed from the Tomb of King Cuo of the Zhongshan State,
Pingshan County, Shijiazhuang City, Hebei Province
Collected by the Cultural Relics Institute of Hebei Province

圆点纹铜双连环
战国中期
长7.2厘米
河北省石家庄市平山县中山王𰻝墓出土
河北省文物研究所藏

铜马衔 | **Bronze *Xian* horse bit**
春秋中晚期 | Middle or Late Spring and Autumn Period
长23.2厘米 | Length 23.2cm
河北省石家庄市平山县访驾庄墓出土 | Unearthed from a tomb at Fangjiazhuang Village, Pingshan County, Shijiazhuang City, Hebei Province
河北省文物研究所藏 | Collected by the Cultural Relics Institute of Hebei Province

铜当卢

战国中期
直径5.3厘米
河北省石家庄市平山县中山王族3号墓出土
河北省文物研究所藏

Bronze *Dang Lu* ornament from a bridle
Middle Warring States Period
Diameter 5.3cm
Unearthed from a Zhongshan noble's tomb No.3, Pingshan County, Shijiazhuang City, Hebei Province
Collected by the Cultural Relics Institute of Hebei Province

○ 圆环形，外附四个小圆环为系带之用。圆环内有两虎，虎四足抓环之内缘，头尾相接，追逐嬉戏。

铜卧兽节约

Bronze crouching beast shaped *Jie Yue* harness fitting
Middle Warring States Period
Length 4.6cm | height 2cm
Unearthed from the Tomb of Duke Cheng of the Zhongshan State, Pingshan County, Shijiazhuang City, Hebei Province
Collected by the Cultural Relics Institute of Hebei Province

:: 战国中期
:: 长4.6厘米 :: 高2厘米
:: 河北省石家庄市平山县中山成公墓二号车马坑出土
:: 河北省文物研究所藏

○ 共出土了10件，器形各不相同。

四虺纠结铜饰

战国中期

长9厘米 ∷ 宽8厘米

河北省石家庄市平山县中山王䰸墓出土

河北省文物研究所藏

Bronze ornament shaped like four coiled *Hui* serpents

Middle Warring States Period
Length 9cm | width 8cm
Unearthed from the Tomb of King Cuo of the Zhongshan State, Pingshan County, Shijiazhuang City, Hebei Province
Collected by the Cultural Relics Institute of Hebei Province

错金银铜车軎

Bronze *Yi* semi-circular fittings from the *Heng* horizontal drawbar of a chariot inlaid with a gold and silver design
Middle Warring States Period
Width 7.6~9cm
Unearthed from the Tomb of Duke Cheng of the Zhongshan State, Pingshan County, Shijiazhuang City, Hebei Province
Collected by the Cultural Relics Institute of Hebei Province

::战国中期
::宽7.6~9厘米
::河北省石家庄市平山县中山成公墓二号车马坑出土
::河北省文物研究所藏

◎ 共出土了1套5件，1大1小，形制相同。车軎身除了嵌入衡木部分外，全身饰金银错勾连卷云纹。

兽首衔环铜插

:: 战国中期
:: 高6.4厘米 :: 筒径2厘米 :: 环径3.4厘米
:: 河北省石家庄市平山县中山成公墓二号车马坑出土
:: 河北省文物研究所藏

○ 共出土了4件，形制大小相同。为车衡上穿缰绳的环插，出土时环插于车衡内。

Bronze insertion component shaped like a beast containing a ring
Middle Warring States Period
Height 6.4cm | diameter of tube 2cm | diameter of ring 3.4cm
Unearthed from the Tomb of Duke Cheng of the Zhongshan State, Pingshan County, Shijiazhuang City, Hebei Province
Collected by the Cultural Relics Institute of Hebei Province

Polychrome bone finial from the *Heng* horizontal drawbar of a chariot

Middle Warring States Period
Length 6cm
Unearthed from the Tomb of King Cuo of the Zhongshan State, Pingshan County, Shijiazhuang City, Hebei Province
Collected by the Cultural Relics Institute of Hebei Province

彩绘骨衡帽

战国中期
长6厘米
河北省石家庄市平山县中山王䰭墓出土
河北省文物研究所藏

错金龙（虎）首形铜衡帽

Gold inlaid bronze dragon head shaped finial from the *Heng* horizontal drawbar of a chariot
Middle Warring States Period
Height 10cm | diameter 3cm
Unearthed from the Tomb of Duke Cheng of the Zhongshan State, Pingshan County, Shijiazhuang City, Hebei Province
Collected by the Cultural Relics Institute of Hebei Province

战国中期
高10厘米 直径3厘米
河北省石家庄市平山县中山成公墓二号车马坑出土
河北省文物研究所藏

共出土了2对4件，形制大小相同，是套入车衡两端之帽。器身为错金银龙首衔环，帽顶铸成夔龙首，双目圆睁，口衔小环，小环内套有一大环。

铜杆首帽

Bronze cap from a shaft
Middle or Late Warring States Period
Length 6.5cm
Unearthed from a Zhongshan noble's tomb No.5, Pingshan County,
Pingshan County, Shijiazhuang City, Hebei Province
Collected by the Cultural Relics Institute of Hebei Province

::战国中晚期
::长6.5厘米
::河北省石家庄市平山县中山国王族5号墓车马坑出土
::河北省文物研究所藏

◎ 中山王族5号墓在中山成公陵之西,属于王陵区内墓葬,有车马坑。据考古专家推测,王族5号墓的主人应是中山成公的弟弟。

龙首形金衡帽

:: 战国中期
:: 长9.8厘米 :: 直径3厘米
:: 河北省石家庄市平山县中山王䦩墓二号车马坑出土
:: 河北省文物研究所藏

◎王车上的构件，用纯金制成。龙首形，龙首长而直，中空。龙额顶饰叶状凸起。双腮饰卷云纹。双目倒立而突出。鼻上三道褶纹，两侧饰卷云纹。吻部前伸，上唇卷起。口部微启，露出交错的牙齿。花叶形双耳、两龙角呈"八"字分开。形象传神，铸造精良。

Gold dragon head shaped fittings from the *Heng*
horizontal drawbar of a chariot

Middle Warring States Period
Length 9.8cm | diameter 3cm
Unearthed from the Tomb of King Cuo of the Zhongshan State, Pingshan County, Shijiazhuang City, Hebei Province
Collected by the Cultural Relics Institute of Hebei Province

双夔兽铜轭帽及轭帽座

战国中期
轭帽通高17.4厘米 :: 夔兽长13厘米
河北省石家庄市平山县中山成公墓出土
河北省文物研究所藏

车器一对，形制与大小相同，轭帽长方形中空，两侧面各铸有圆雕夔兽一只，夔兽攀爬于立柱之上，双耳直立，双目圆睁，尾巴上卷，回首怒吼，极富动感，轭帽前后两面均饰卷云纹，上部有方形穿，以插入木楗使之固定在轭上。轭帽座为菱形，中空，顶面平整，器身弧收，前后两面饰浮雕纠结蟠蛇纹，其上面安插轭帽，下面连接铜管。

A pair of bronze fittings with double *Kui* dragon shaped decoration on the yoke

Middle Warring States Period
Full height 17.4cm
Length of *Kui* dragon decoration 13cm
Unearthed from the Tomb of Duke Cheng of the Zhongshan State, Pingshan County, Shijiazhuang City, Hebei Province
Collected by the Cultural Relics Institute of Hebei Province

金轭首饰

战国中期
高4.5厘米
河北省石家庄市平山县中山王䰜墓二号车马坑出土
河北省文物研究所藏

Gold ornament from the tip of a yoke
Middle Warring States Period
Height 4.5cm
Unearthed from the Tomb of King Cuo of the Zhongshan State,
Pingshan County, Shijiazhuang City, Hebei Province
Collected by the Cultural Relics Institute of Hebei Province

金轭首，直筒状，一头略细，另一头有銎口，銎口边起棱，器侧有两销钉孔。

金轭鈎饰

::战国中期
::长8.1厘米
::河北省石家庄市平山县中山王𰯼墓二号车马坑出土
::河北省文物研究所藏

◎体弯曲呈勾状，两侧有立边，正面平，呈长圆形，侧面弧曲，上下各有一道凸棱饰。下端有三齿销钉孔用于镶嵌固定。

Gold ornaments from the ends of a yoke
Middle Warring States Period
Length 8.1cm
Unearthed from the Tomb of King Cuo of the Zhongshan State,
Pingshan County, Shijiazhuang City, Hebei Province
Collected by the Cultural Relics Institute of Hebei Province

Bronze pole caps inlaid with silver

Middle Warring States Period
Height 12.8cm | diameter of pole 3.1cm | diameter of bell 5.2cm
Unearthed from the Pit for Boats in the Tomb of King Cuo of the Zhongshan State, Pingshan County, Shijiazhuang City, Hebei Province
Collected by the Cultural Relics Institute of Hebei Province

错银铜杆顶帽

战国中期
均高12.8厘米∷銎径3.1厘米∷铃径5.2厘米
河北省石家庄市平山县中山王譻墓葬船坑出土
河北省文物研究所藏

Bronze bell

Middle Warring States Period
Height 3.1cm
Unearthed from Pit 1 of Chariots and Horses in the Tomb of Duke Cheng of the Zhongshan State, Pingshan County, Shijiazhuang City, Hebei Province
Collected by the Cultural Relics Institute of Hebei Province

铜铃
::: 战国中期
::: 高3.1厘米
::: 河北省石家庄市平山县中山成公墓一号车马坑出土
::: 河北省文物研究所藏

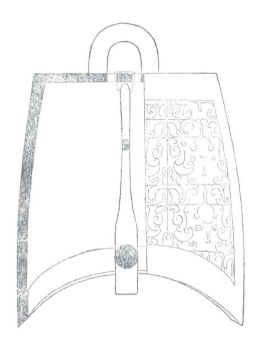

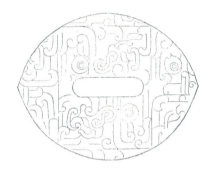

铜铎

- 战国中期
- 高10.9厘米
- 河北省石家庄市平山县中山王䰜墓出土
- 河北省文物研究所藏

军阵乐器，振铎击鼓，鼓舞士气。形似钮钟，顶部有两孔以系舌。铎表面纹饰繁复，顶面为重云纹，器身为云雷纹。纹线细密清晰，刻工精巧。

Bronze *Duo* bell

Middle Warring States Period
Height 10.9cm
Unearthed from the Tomb of King Cuo of the Zhongshan State,
Pingshan County, Shijiazhuang City, Hebei Province
Collected by the Cultural Relics Institute of Hebei Province

Bronze *Ge* dagger-axe head with gold shank
Middle Warring States Period
Shank length 21.2cm | shank diameter 4.4cm | *Ge* length 20.1cm
Unearthed from the Tomb of King Cuo of the Zhongshan State,
Pingshan County, Shijiazhuang City, Hebei Province
Collected by the Cultural Relics Institute of Hebei Province

金镈铜戈
::战国中期
::镈长21.2厘米 ::上径4.4厘米 ::戈长20.1厘米
::河北省石家庄市平山县中山王𦉢墓出土
::河北省文物研究所藏

出土了形制相同的两件金镈铜戈，镈为纯金打造，重达902克，镈上饰两条龙，用银和蓝琉璃镶嵌龙眼，用白银镶出树枝状龙角、双翼。造型奇巧，工艺精湛。

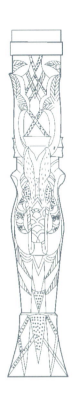

蟠虺纠结纹铜剑

Bronze sword with intertwined *Pan Hui* serpant pattern
Spring and Autumn Period to Early Warring States Period
Length 31.7cm
Unearthed from a tomb at Fangjiazhuang Village, Pingshan County,
Shijiazhuang City, Hebei Province
Collected by the Cultural Relics Institute of Hebei Province

:: 春秋至战国早期
:: 长31.7厘米
:: 河北省石家庄市平山县访驾庄墓出土
:: 河北省文物研究所藏

◎ 剑身细长，脊高起，两侧有一凹槽。柄中空，其上镂雕蟠虺纠结纹。铜质精良，工艺细腻。

矢箙（箭袋）配件

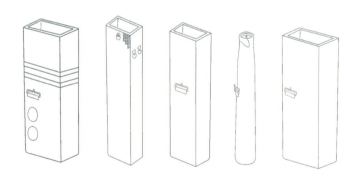

矢箙复原示意图

矢箙，盛箭之器。《周礼·夏官·司弓矢》中郑注云：「箙，盛矢器也，以兽皮为之。」兽皮已失，只剩铜配件，有铜卡环、包银铜泡饰、铜铺首、铜吊环、银盖。泡饰为箙套外的装饰物；卡环中间均竖一鸭首状卡针，可将箙套挂在环形带上；铜铺首和吊环均系结箙套之用；银盖为箙套上部的封盖。

Bronze silver coated oblate ornament form a quiver
Middle Warring States Period
Diameter 8.5cm
Unearthed from the Tomb of King Cuo of the Zhongshan State,
Pingshan County, Shijiazhuang City, Hebei Province
Collected by the Cultural Relics Institute of Hebei Province

矢箙包银铜泡饰
::战国中期
::直径8.5厘米
::河北省石家庄市平山县中山王䰅墓出土
::河北省文物研究所藏

Bronze knocker part from a quiver
Middle Warring States Period
Height of Beast 2.4cm
Unearthed from the Tomb of King Cuo of the Zhongshan State,
Pingshan County, Shijiazhuang City, Hebei Province
Collected by the Cultural Relics Institute of Hebei Province

矢箙铜铺首
::战国中期
::兽面高2.4厘米
::河北省石家庄市平山县中山王䰅墓出土
::河北省文物研究所藏

Bronze ring part form a quiver
Middle Warring States Period
Diameter 2.6cm
Unearthed from the Tomb of King Cuo of the Zhongshan State,
Pingshan County, Shijiazhuang City, Hebei Province
Collected by the Cultural Relics Institute of Hebei Province

矢箙铜吊环
::战国中期
::环径2.6厘米
::河北省石家庄市平山县中山王䰅墓出土
::河北省文物研究所藏

Silver cover of a quiver
Middle Warring States Period
Diameter 6.2cm
Unearthed from the Tomb of King Cuo of the Zhongshan State, Pingshan County, Shijiazhuang City, Hebei Province
Collected by the Cultural Relics Institute of Hebei Province

矢箙银盖
::战国中期
::直径6.2厘米
::河北省石家庄市平山县中山王䰅墓出土
::河北省文物研究所藏

Bronze ring part from a quiver
Middle Warring States Period
Length 10.5cm
Unearthed from the Tomb of King Cuo of the Zhongshan State, Pingshan County, Shijiazhuang City, Hebei Province
Collected by the Cultural Relics Institute of Hebei Province

矢箙长方形铜卡环
::战国中期
::长10.5厘米
::河北省石家庄市平山县中山王䰅墓出土
::河北省文物研究所藏

三棱铜镞 | **Triangular bronze arrowheads**
战国中期 | Middle Warring States Period
连铤长10~31厘米 | Length (with shank) 10~31cm
河北省石家庄市平山县中山王䰉墓出土 | Unearthed from the Tomb of King Cuo of the Zhongshan State,
河北省文物研究所藏 | Pingshan County, Shijiazhuang City, Hebei Province
 | Collected by the Cultural Relics Institute of Hebei Province

Arrowheads with round tips

Middle Warring States Period
Length(with shank) 6.7cm
Unearthed from the Tomb of King Cuo of the Zhongshan State,
Pingshan County, Shijiazhuang City, Hebei Province
Collected by the Cultural Relics Institute of Hebei Province

圆头铜镞

::战国中期
::连铤长6.7厘米
::河北省石家庄市平山县中山王䰭墓出土
::河北省文物研究所藏

包金镶银铜泡饰

Bronze gold coated oblate ornaments inlaid with a silver design
Middle Warring States Period
Diameter 5.2~5.8cm | weight 60~80g
Unearthed from the Tomb of King Cuo of the Zhongshan State, Pingshan County, Shijiazhuang City, Hebei Province
Collected by the Cultural Relics Institute of Hebei Province

战国中期
直径5.2~5.8厘米 ∷ 重60~80克
河北省石家庄市平山县中山王䰜墓出土
河北省文物研究所藏

◎ 共出土4件。此件出土于北盗洞。整体呈圆形，外圈鼓棱，包金片，中心镶嵌用银片捶打成的梅花，精巧秀丽。

夔龙纹镶金银泡饰

:: 直径5.3厘米 :: 重86克
:: 河北省石家庄市平山县中山王䰜墓出土
:: 河北省文物研究所藏

Bronze oblate ornament inlaid with a gold and silver *Kui* dragon pattern
Middle Warring States Period
Diameter 5.3cm | weight 86g
Unearthed from the Tomb of King Cuo of the Zhongshan State, Pingshan County, Shijiazhuang City, Hebei Province
Collected by the Cultural Relics Institute of Hebei Province

中山王䰜墓出土各类泡饰24件，有银质镶金的、有铜质包金、铜质包金镶银、铜质素面的，有的出土时背面尚存朽革，应是革甲上的饰物。

这件银质镶金泡饰保存完好，圆形，凸面。外缘针刺锯齿纹，凸面装饰两只缠绕扭结的夔龙，中心镶铸一朵柿蒂形金花。金花花瓣上有针刺叶脉和点纹。背面为四个短柱体承托一方形环，铸有铭文一周，为「十三祀，私库，啬夫煮正，工孟鲜」12字。

中山侯铜钺

:: 战国中期
:: 长29.4厘米 :: 宽25.5厘米
:: 河北省石家庄市平山县中山王䲨墓出土
:: 河北省文物研究所藏

Bronze *Yue* halberd belonging to Marquis Zhongshan

Middle Warring States Period
Length 29.4cm ǀ width 25.5cm
Unearthed from the Tomb of King Cuo of the Zhongshan State,
Pingshan County, Shijiazhuang City, Hebei Province
Collected by the Cultural Relics Institute of Hebei Province

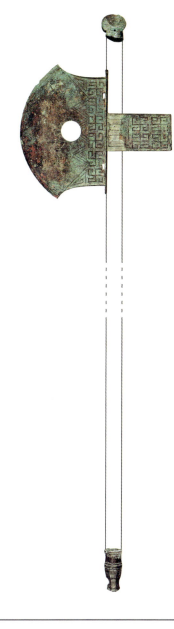

中山侯钺铭文

Rubbing of the Inscription on the Bronze *Yue* halberd

天子建邦，中山侯恣。兹作军钺，以敬（警）氒（厥）众。

中山侯钺铭文

中山王䰠墓出土，是中山国称侯的象征。钺是古代的兵器，也是象征王权的礼器。这件铜钺上刻有铭文2行16字，铭文内容为：「天子建邦，中山侯恣（yīn）。作兹军钺，以敬（警）氒（厥）众。」意为中山侯受命于周天子，其威严不可侵犯。一起展示的还有铜钺柲之两端的铜帽和铜镈。

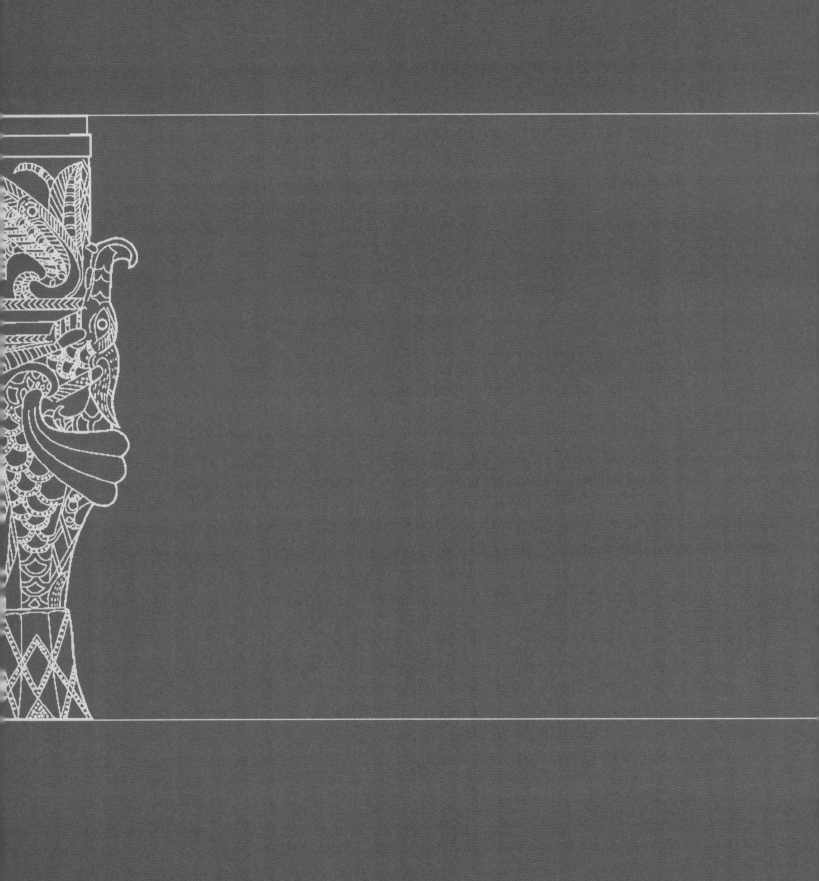

Five Part: Mausoleum of the Kings of the Zhongshan State

Although the Zhongshan State existed a very long time ago, the mausoleum complex of the kings of the state with its magnificent layout, great size, and rich burial objects shows us the past brilliance of the Zhongshan. The mausoleum is composed of two parts: one is in the northern part of west Lingshou city; another is outside western Lingshou city. Many tombs of nobles have been discovered in the mausoleum complex: two of which have been excavated. Given their layout and the burial objects found within these tombs, Tomb M1 is assumed to be that of King Cuo while Tomb M6 is probably that of Duke Cheng. Both tombs are stone tombs shaped like the Chinese character *Zhong*（中） and each contains a warehouse holding funerary objects. Although both the central burial chambers of the tombs had been looted in antiquity, archaeologists were still able to uncover hundreds of precious artefacts in the warehouses.

第五部分 中山王陵

春秋战国那个异彩纷呈的时代，距离我们太过遥远。中山王陵以规模宏大、布局严谨、埋藏丰富成为中山国历史文化的真实载体，昭示着这个诸侯国曾经的辉煌。中山王陵区有两处，分别位于灵寿古城西城北部和西城之外。1974年至1978年，对其中的两座王墓进行了发掘，根据对墓葬形制和出土器物的研究推断M1为中山王𰯼墓，M6为中山成公墓。中山成公墓和中山王𰯼墓均为『中』字形积石墓，设有存放随葬品的库室。两墓主室已被盗空，库室内却出土了大量珍贵文物。

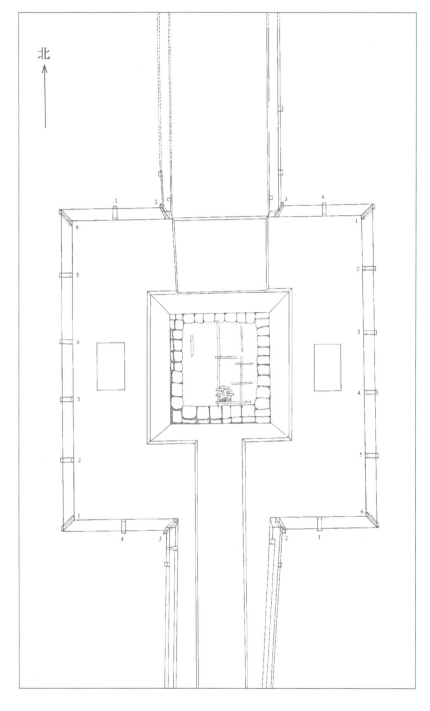

中山成公墓平面图

中山成公墓

中山成公墓由墓道、墓室、椁室、两个库室和两个车马坑组成,另有三座陪葬墓。墓上封土高大,原有享堂建筑。

中山成公墓发掘现场

中山成公墓墓室全景

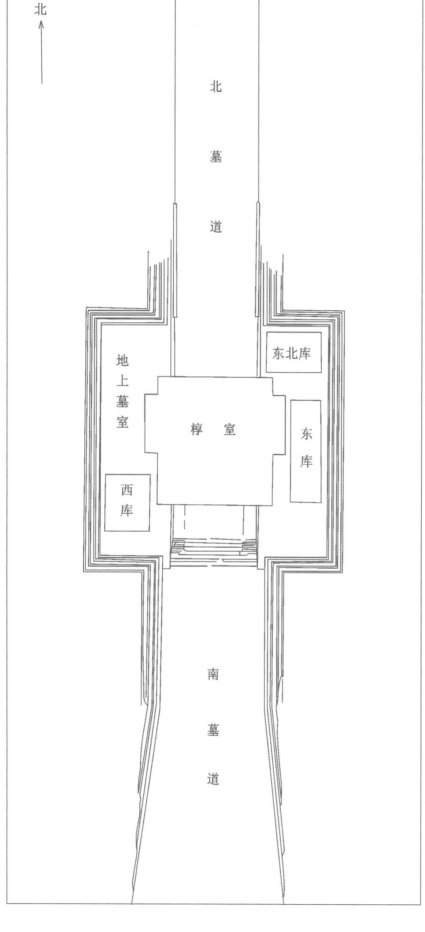

中山王䰷墓墓室平面图

中山王䰷墓

◎ 中山王䰷墓是中山国墓葬中最大的一座，为"中"字形积石墓，由南北墓道、墓室、椁室和三个库室组成，周围有两个车马坑、一个杂殉坑、一个葬船坑及六座陪葬墓。墓上原有高大的封土，上面建有享堂建筑。

中山王𫲧墓东库东南角遗物

中山王𫲧墓东库南部遗物

中山王𫲧墓西库西南部遗物

中山王𫲧墓西库玉器

中山王𫲧墓西库铜编钟、石磬等

中山王䝮墓

◎ 中山王䝮墓的独特之处，在于它设有"库室"，许多珍贵物品都埋藏在库室中，躲过了盗墓者的劫掠，从而让我们今天能够欣赏到中山国的众多文物珍品。

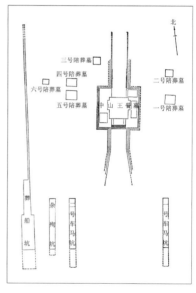

中山王䝮墓葬船坑全景　　　　　　　　　　中山王䝮墓葬船坑位置示意图

◎ 中山王䝮墓的葬船坑在北方墓葬中极为罕见，葬船坑的北面挖有一条长沟象征河道。坑内分为南北两室，南室原并列放有三条大船，北室原放有彩漆的主船。

中山王䝮墓及哀后墓墓丘

中山王墓发掘现场

中山王墓墓室全景

中山王墓发掘现场

中山王墓东库中部遗物

◎ 错金银铜版兆域图是迄今发现的世界上最早的有比例的铜版建筑规划图,为研究我国古代陵园规划和建筑图学提供了珍贵而准确的资料。铜版为中山王䰠陵区的建筑规划图,指示方向为上南、下北。图版的中心部位用金片嵌出五个享堂的轮廓线,有王堂、哀后堂、王后堂和两个夫人堂。享堂的外围,用银丝标识墓的封土底边——丘𫮃(qiàn)。再向外,用宽银片嵌出"内宫垣"和"中宫垣"二层宫墙轮廓线,其中内宫垣的北部嵌有"诏宗宫""正奎宫""执帛宫"和"大将宫"的标识,分别是陵园中主持祭祀礼仪、主管清洁、主管祭祀用品和看守陵墓的官员处所。还在图中标示各个建筑的长度和间距,换算后得知图版的比例为1∶500。王堂上部铸有国王命令修建陵墓的诏书。

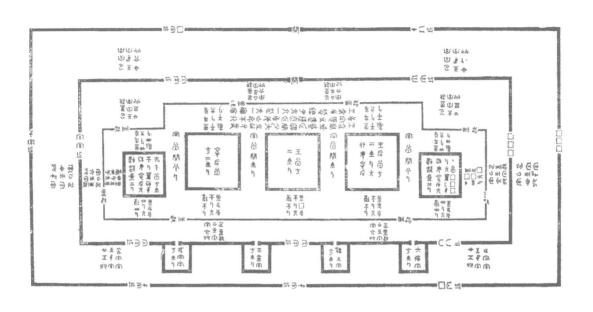

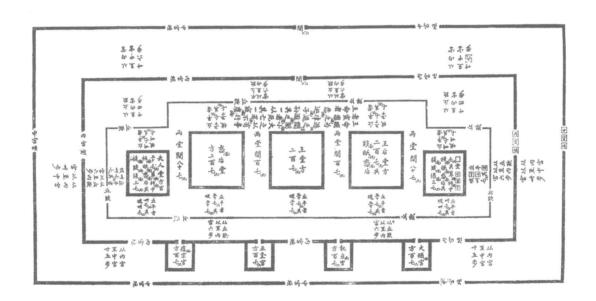

守丘刻石

Shouqiu stone with inscriptions
Length 90cm | width 50cm | thickness 40cm
Collected by the Cultural Relics Institute of Hebei Province

∷ 长90厘米 ∷ 宽50厘米 ∷ 厚40厘米
∷ 河北省文物研究所藏

◎ 1935年，一位农民在平山县下七汲村西南发现一块大河光石，石上刻有19个字，证实这一带为中山国王陵和都城所在地。

◎ 铭文："监罟尤臣公乘得守丘，亓（其）白（旧）将曼敢谒后卡（俶）贤者。"

◎ 铭文释意：监管捕鱼的罪臣公乘得在此看守陵墓，他的旧将曼敬告后来善良贤德的人。

铁足铜鼎

∷ 战国中期
∷ 通高51.5厘米 ∷ 口径42厘米 ∷ 重60千克
∷ 河北省石家庄市平山县中山王䰇墓出土
∷ 河北省文物研究所藏

Bronze *Ding* tripod with iron feet
Middle Warring States Period
Height 51.5cm | mouth diameter 42cm | weight 60kg
Unearthed from the Tomb of King Cuo of the Zhongshan State,
Pingshan County, Shijiazhuang City, Hebei Province
Collected by the Cultural Relics Institute of Hebei Province

◎ 中山王䰇墓出土九鼎中的首鼎。鼎带盖，盖面有三个等距云形钮。鼎体略呈扁圆形，鼓腹，三蹄形足。鼎为铜身铁足，是一件铜铁合铸器。出土时鼎内残存结晶状肉羹，底部有火烧烟迹。鼎的外壁刻有铭文77行，共计469字，是目前发现的铭文最长的战国时期青铜器。铭文记载了中山国相邦司马赒率领军队伐燕国、开疆扩土的史实，告诫后代要吸取燕国"子之之乱"的历史教训，并警惕周边诸国的进攻，为研究中山国提供了重要的史料。鼎上的铭文刀法娴熟流畅，笔画刚劲洗炼，文辞典雅优美，是欣赏和研究战国文字和书法的珍贵资料。

犀足蟠螭纹铜筒形器

:: 战国中期
:: 高58.5厘米 :: 口径24.5厘米
:: 河北省石家庄市平山县中山王䰠墓出土
:: 河北省文物研究所藏

◎ 器身为直筒形，平底。器表面满饰盘曲环绕的蟠螭纹和雷纹，中腰部位有一道宽带纹，宽带纹上方的两侧各有一只兽面衔环铺首。器足为三只周身刻卷云纹的犀牛，昂首张目，用力撑起筒身。犀牛与筒身的焊接严丝合缝。器物的具体用途不详，内外均无烧熏痕迹，也无盛用食物的痕迹，可能是投壶或温酒器。

Bronze cylindrical vessel with *Pan Chi* coiled serpent pattern
Middle Warring States Period
Height 58.5cm I mouth diameter 24.5cm
Unearthed from the Tomb of King Cuo of the Zhongshan State, Pingshan County, Shijiazhuang City, Hebei Province
Collected by the Cultural Relics Institute of Hebei Province

夔龙纹饰铜方壶

:: 战国中期
:: 通高63厘米 :: 腹径35厘米 :: 重28.72千克
:: 河北省石家庄市平山县中山王䰠墓出土
:: 河北省文物研究所藏

Bronze *Hu* wine jar with *Kui* dragon pattern
Middle Warring States Period
Height 63cm ǀ belly diameter 35cm ǀ weight 28.72kg
Unearthed from the Tomb of King Cuo of the Zhongshan State, Pingshan County, Shijiazhuang City, Hebei Province
Collected by the Cultural Relics Institute of Hebei Province

酒器和礼器，盝顶形盖，盖顶四面坡各有一个镂空云形钮，壶为直口，短颈，溜肩，鼓腹，平底，高圈足。壶身周正，棱角分明，四角的肩部各铸有一条神采飞扬、昂首攀爬的立体夔龙。壶腹两侧各有一个兽面衔环铺首，兽面狰狞，双睛倒竖，眉须涡卷。壶的四周刻有流畅优美的铭文450字，是一篇优秀的战国书法作品。据铭文记载：中山王䰠十四年，中山伐燕获胜后，用燕国的青铜器熔铸此壶。铭文颂扬了中山伐燕的战绩，阐述了巩固政权和立国安邦的道理，其中特别提到了「皇祖文武、桓祖成考」等中山国国君的名号，填补了史籍中关于中山国国君世系记录的缺漏。

银首人俑铜灯

::: 战国中期
::: 通高66.4厘米
::: 河北省石家庄市平山县中山王𰯼墓出土
::: 河北省文物研究所藏

Bronze lamp supported by a human figure
Middle Warring States Period
Height 66.4cm
Unearthed from the Tomb of King Cuo of the Zhongshan State, Pingshan County, Shijiazhuang City, Hebei Province
Collected by the Cultural Relics Institute of Hebei Province

◎ 灯由人俑、蛇、灯杆、灯盘和方座组成。人俑的头为银制,眼珠为黑宝石镶嵌,发型精致,胡须微翘,笑容可掬,表情生动。人俑着云纹右衽宽袖锦袍,腰间系有带钩,广袖低垂,风度潇洒。他右手握住一蛇,蛇首上挺,用吻部托住长长的灯柱。柱面装饰着夔龙戏猴纹饰;左手握一蛇的尾部、蛇身卷曲,头部昂起,吻部顶着一只灯盘。在底部灯盘内还有一蛇盘踞,以头顶住男子左手所握之蛇,保证了全灯的重心稳定。此灯的三个灯盘内各有三个灯签,点亮时烛光灯影上下辉映,令人赏心悦目。

十五连盏铜灯

::战国中期
::高82.9厘米 ::底径26厘米
::河北省石家庄市平山县中山王譻墓出土
::河北省文物研究所藏

Bronze lamp with fifteen fuel chambers
Middle Warring States Period
Height 82.9cm | base diameter 26cm
Unearthed from the Tomb of King Cuo of the Zhongshan State,
Pingshan County, Shijiazhuang City, Hebei Province
Collected by the Cultural Relics Institute of Hebei Province

◎ 出土一件。灯的整体造型仿佛一棵大树，十五条枝头托十五只灯盘，高低有序、错落有致。灯体分八节，每节的榫头形状各异，便于安装。树干上盘绕三条螭龙，树枝间小鸟引颈鸣叫，群猴嬉戏玩耍。三只独首双身的猛虎托起圆形底座，底座上两男俑正抛食戏猴。这盏灯设计科学，造型别致，人与动物和谐相处，妙趣横生，是不可多得的文物珍品。

◎ 在灯底座侧面和灯柱上有铭文：「十祀，左使车（厍），啬夫事斁（yi），工弧，冢（重）一石三百五十五刀之冢（重）。右䝼者。」

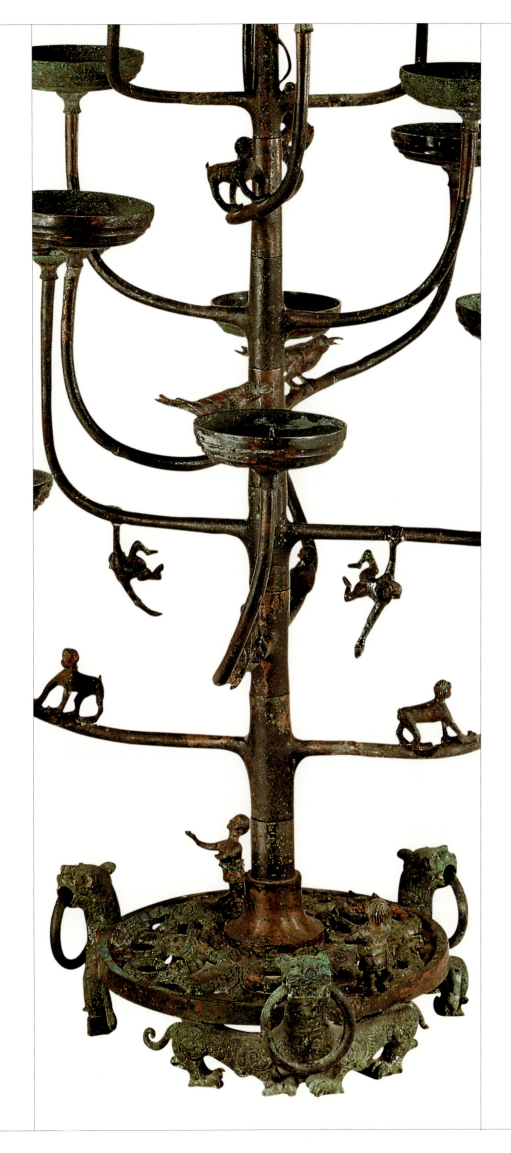

鸟柱铜盆

Bronze basin with a post topped by a bird finial
Middle Warring States Period
Height 47.5cm | diameter 57cm
Unearthed from the Tomb of King Cuo of the Zhongshan State,
Pingshan County, Shijiazhuang City, Hebei Province
Collected by the Cultural Relics Institute of Hebei Province

::战国中期
::高47.5厘米 :: 盆径57厘米
::河北省石家庄市平山县中山王䰜墓出土
::河北省文物研究所藏

水器或陈设器，盆壁直立，盆底有束腰型圆柱承托，柱下有圆形圈座。盆内底中间伏有一只龟，龟背上竖有一根圆柱，柱顶站立一只可转动的飞鸟，鸟的双爪紧紧抓住两只纠结的蛇头，鸟作展翅飞翔状，羽毛丰满，引颈长鸣，形象逼真。盆的外壁装饰四只衔圆环的飞鸟，底座镂雕活泼的螭纹，圈足上有铭文："八祀，冶匀（钧）䰜夫孙蕊，工酋。"表明该器做于王䰜八年。

椁室铜铺首

战国中期
面宽16.2厘米 :: 高9.6厘米 :: 环径12.8厘米
榫长11厘米 :: 高8.2厘米
河北省石家庄市平山县中山王䰠墓出土
河北省文物研究所藏

Bronze knocker on the *Guo* outer coffin
Middle Warring States Period
Width 16.2cm | height 9.6cm | diameter of ring 12.8cm
length of tenon 11cm | height 8.2cm
Unearthed from the Tomb of King Cuo of the Zhongshan State, Pingshan County, Shijiazhuang City, Hebei Province
Collected by the Cultural Relics Institute of Hebei Province

○ 中山王䰠墓共出土44件铺首,此件是外椁上的八铺首之一。铺首兽面衔环,铺首后有长榫,便于嵌入棺板。

细孔流铜鼎

Bronze *Ding* tripod with a ten-hole spout
Middle Warring States Period
Height 21.6cm | diameter of Mouth 21cm
Unearthed from the Tomb of King Cuo of the Zhongshan State,
Pingshan County, Shijiazhuang City, Hebei Province
Collected by the Cultural Relics Institute of Hebei Province

∷ 战国中期
∷ 通高21.6厘米∷口径21厘米
∷ 河北省石家庄市平山县中山王䰜墓出土
∷ 河北省文物研究所藏

鼎带盖，子口内敛，两侧有长方形附耳，腹稍鼓，平底，三蹄形足。盖为平顶，顶面有三个等距环形钮。鼎腹中部有一道凸弦纹。上腹一侧有流，流上作10个细孔，流在倒汤时起过滤作用，可防止杂物流出。出土时鼎内底部残存结晶状肉羹。此种样式的鼎在国内属首次发现。鼎腹凸弦纹下面有铭文：「左使車（库），工蔡。」

钮钟

战国中期
高5.8~6.8厘米
河北省石家庄市平山县中山王𰯼墓葬船坑出土
河北省文物研究所藏

因葬船坑盗扰严重，只发掘3件。此3件依照原套钮钟顺序列于中间。钮身饰云雷纹，篆部饰雷纹，枚有云雷纹地，钲和鼓饰云雷兽面纹、花纹十分细腻。云雷兽面纹富有神秘气息。

***Bronze Niu* knob bell**

Middle Warring States Period
Height 5.8~6.8cm
Unearthed from the Pit of Boats in the Tomb of King Cuo of the Zhongshan State, Pingshan County, Shijiazhuang City, Hebei Province
Collected by the Cultural Relics Institute of Hebei Province

葬船坑铜钮钟尺寸统计表

单位：厘米

器号	顺序号	钮高	铣长	舞广	舞修	鼓间	铣间	唇厚	重量（公斤）
ZCK:1	1	6.8	15.3	7.2	9.6	9.4	12	1	2.65
ZCK:2	2	6	14	6.9	8.9	8.6	11.1	0.8	2.05
ZCK:3	3	5.8	12.9	6.3	8.2	8.1	10.6	0.8	1.85

灰黑陶鸭形尊

战国中期

通高30.6厘米 ∷ 长42.5厘米 ∷ 腹径21.3厘米

河北省石家庄市平山县中山成公墓出土

河北省文物研究所藏

明器。泥质灰黑陶，整器呈鸭形。鸭，伸头、屈颈，扁球形腹，板状尾，平板双足。背上高盖钮，盖顶一鸟。器身通体磨光，压划出卷云纹、弦纹内填曲齿纹等。

Dark grey pottery duck shaped *Zun* vessel

Middle Warring States Period
Full height 30.6cm | length 42.5cm | belly diameter 21.3cm
Unearthed from the Tomb of Duke Cheng of the Zhongshan State,
Pingshan County, Shijiazhuang City, Hebei Province
Collected by the Cultural Relics Institute of Hebei Province

灰黑陶盖豆

战国中期
高28.2厘米 ∷ 腹径20.8厘米 ∷ 口径18.4厘米
河北省石家庄市平山县中山成公墓出土
河北省文物研究所藏

◎ 共出土4件。明器。泥质灰黑陶，覆钵形盖，上有圆饼形的捉手。器身子口内敛，鼓腹，短柄，喇叭形假圈足。整器通体磨光，盖上饰凸弦纹，腹部饰有「S」形暗纹宽带一周，器足满饰弦纹。

Dark grey pottery *Dou* with a cover
Middle Warring States Period
Height 28.2cm | belly diameter 20.8cm | mouth diameter 18.4cm
Unearthed from the Tomb of Duke Cheng of the Zhongshan State,
Pingshan County, Shijiazhuang City, Hebei Province
Collected by the Cultural Relics Institute of Hebei Province

磨光压划纹黑陶盖豆

战国中期
高33.9厘米
河北省石家庄市平山县中山王䝮陪葬墓出土
河北省文物研究所藏

Polished black pottery covered *Dou* with a scratched design
Middle Warring States Period
Height 33.9cm
Unearthed from the ancillary Tomb of King Cuo of the Zhongshan State,
Pingshan County, Shijiazhuang City, Hebei Province
Collected by the Cultural Relics Institute of Hebei Province

◎ 明器。覆钵形盖，圆饼形捉手，器身子口内敛，鼓腹，圜底，细柄，喇叭形座，平底。通体磨光，盖面饰弦纹间以三角形，内填波折纹。豆身为卷云纹，内填波折纹、弦纹等。底座面为卷云纹填横线纹和三角形，内填波折纹。

磨光压划纹黑陶甗

战国中期
高31.9厘米
河北省石家庄市平山县中山王𰯼墓出土
河北省文物研究所藏

Polished black pottery *Yan* steamer with a scratched design
Middle Warring States Period
Height 31.9cm
Unearthed from the Tomb of King Cuo of the Zhongshan State, Pingshan County, Shijiazhuang City, Hebei Province
Collected by the Cultural Relics Institute of Hebei Province

甗,上部为甑,下部为鼎足鬲。甑,宽平沿,侈口,腹内收,外附两环耳,下接鬲。鬲圆肩,鼓腹、圜底、三蹄形足,肩侧有两环耳。通体磨光,黑亮。器表压划纹饰密集,有弦纹、兽纹、卷云纹,内填波折纹等。

磨光压划纹黑陶陶碗

::战国中期
::口径19.6厘米
::河北省石家庄市平山县中山王𦮘墓出土
::河北省文物研究所藏

◎ 敛口，深鼓腹，圆底，小圈足。通体磨光，压划凹弦纹、卷云纹内填波折纹、交叉［S］纹等。

Polished black pottery bowl with a scratched design
Middle Warring States Period
Diameter 19.6cm
Unearthed from the Tomb of King Cuo of Zhongshan State, Pingshan County, Shijiazhuang City, Hebei Province
Collected by the Cultural Relics Institute of Hebei Province

享堂陶筒瓦及瓦钉饰

::战国中期
::筒瓦长90厘米 :: 瓦钉饰高42厘米
::河北省石家庄市平山县中山王䜽墓出土
::河北省文物研究所藏

○陵墓享堂建筑构件。瓦身为半圆筒形，表面饰绳纹。前有圆形瓦当，后背方形钉孔，上面安插有瓦钉，瓦钉饰呈花叶状。筒瓦的尾部有子口，可与后瓦相衔接。

Clay barrel tile and tile nail ornament from the Memorial Hall
Middle Warring States Period
Length of tile 90cm l height of nail 42cm
Unearthed from the Tomb of King Cuo of the Zhongshan State, Pingshan County, Shijiazhuang City, Hebei Province
Collected by the Cultural Relics Institute of Hebei Province

平体龙形青玉佩

::战国中期
::长21.3厘米
::河北省石家庄市平山县中山王䰖墓出土
::河北省文物研究所藏

青玉质,灰绿色,半透明。龙形。龙身呈拱形,回首长吻贴后背。尾分岔上卷贴背,与长吻相呼应。四足。背中部靠上有一穿。有边廓,阴刻涡纹。

Sapphire dragon shaped *Pei* pendant
Middle Warring States Period
Length 21.3cm
Unearthed from the Tomb of King Cuo of the Zhongshan State,
Pingshan County, Shijiazhuang City, Hebei Province
Collected by the Cultural Relics Institute of Hebei Province

弧背龙形青玉佩

Sapphire dragon shaped *Pei* pendant
Middle Warring States Period
Length 8.9cm
Unearthed from the Tomb of King Cuo of the Zhongshan State,
Pingshan County, Shijiazhuang City, Hebei Province
Collected by the Cultural Relics Institute of Hebei Province

::战国中期
::长8.9厘米
::河北省石家庄市平山县中山王䰼墓出土
::河北省文物研究所藏

玉色青灰，半透明。龙首部宽大，有前伸上折的短角，口如猪嘴，长吻前伸，下唇短平。背上中部有一穿孔。有边廓，两面阴线刻卷云纹。

弓体回首龙形青玉佩

::战国中期
::长14.2厘米 ::宽3厘米 ::厚0.6厘米
::河北省石家庄市平山县中山王䰚墓出土
::河北省文物研究所藏

○ 此形制共出土2件，出土于西库。玉色灰绿，质细，半透明，龙形。龙曲体，呈回首奔跑状，长吻上卷与背部相连接，下唇内勾，前伸一足。背中部脊上有一穿。阴线数道长纹勾勒出龙形。

Sapphire dragon shaped *Pei* pendant
Middle Warring States Period
Length14.2cm | width 3cm | thickness 0.6cm
Unearthed from the Tomb of King Cuo of the Zhongshan State,
Pingshan County, Shijiazhuang City, Hebei Province
Collected by the Cultural Relics Institute of Hebei Province

弓体卷尾龙形白玉佩

战国中期
长8.3厘米
河北省石家庄市平山县中山王䰜墓出土
河北省文物研究所藏

龙形佩共出土144件。白玉质,黄褐色。龙口微张,尖耳微翘。菱形眼,后尾分岔上翘。背中部靠上有一穿。有廓,两面雕饰谷纹。

White jade dragon shaped *Pei* pendant

Middle Warring States Period
Length 8.3cm
Unearthed from the Tomb of King Cuo of the Zhongshan State, Pingshan County, Pingshan County, Shijiazhuang City, Hebei Province
Collected by the Cultural Relics Institute of Hebei Province

新月形墨玉眼盖

::战国中期
::长3.3厘米 ::厚0.2厘米
::河北省石家庄市平山县中山王譻墓出土
::河北省文物研究所藏

◎ 出土于椁室内。墨玉制，无纹饰。

Jade crescent shaped dark goggles
Middle Warring States Period
Length 3.3cm | thickness 0.2cm
Unearthed from the Tomb of King Cuo of the Zhongshan State,
Pingshan County, Shijiazhuang City, Hebei Province
Collected by the Cultural Relics Institute of Hebei Province

八棱墨玉鼻塞

::战国中期
::长1.8厘米
::河北省石家庄市平山县中山王譻墓出土
::河北省文物研究所藏

Jade octagonal nose plugs
Middle Warring States Period
Length 1.8cm
Unearthed from the Tomb of King Cuo of the Zhongshan State,
Pingshan County, Shijiazhuang City, Hebei Province
Collected by the Cultural Relics Institute of Hebei Province

舌形青玉器

::战国中期
::长2.3厘米
::河北省石家庄市平山县中山王譻陪葬墓出土
::河北省文物研究所藏

Sappire togue shaped artefact
Middle Warring States Period
Length 2.3cm
Unearthed from the Tomb of King Cuo of the Zhongshan State,
Pingshan County, Shijiazhuang City, Hebei Province
Collected by the Cultural Relics Institute of Hebei Province

Sappire earplugs
Middle Warring States Period
Length 5.3cm
Unearthed from the Tomb of King Cuo of the Zhongshan State, Pingshan County, Shijiazhuang City, Hebei Province
Collected by the Cultural Relics Institute of Hebei Province

青玉耳瑱
:: 战国中期
:: 长5.3厘米
:: 河北省石家庄市平山县中山王䰭陪葬墓出土
:: 河北省文物研究所藏

Jade finger covers
Middle Warring States Period
Length 2.2~3.35cm
Unearthed from the Tomb of King Cuo of the Zhongshan State, Pingshan County, Shijiazhuang City, Hebei Province
Collected by the Cultural Relics Institute of Hebei Province

玉手指盖
:: 战国中期
:: 长2.2~3.35厘米
:: 河北省石家庄市平山县中山王䰭墓出土
:: 河北省文物研究所藏

共出土4对8件。春秋战国时期，贵族死后流行厚葬，"含珠鳞施"。"鳞施"即在死者身上覆盖如同鱼鳞的玉片，是汉代玉衣殓葬的前奏。

长条形兽纹石刻板

::战国中期
::长45.4厘米::宽5.3厘米::厚0.4厘米
::河北省石家庄市平山县中山王族3号墓出土
::河北省文物研究所藏

◎共出土8块。青石板长条形。阴刻剔地勾勒出两排8个长方框，每框内浮雕一龙形兽，兽有头、角、尾、爪和弯曲的长身，身上刻鳞片纹。上下两两成对，有的头尾相对，有的首尾相追，形态相类而有别。该墓还出土呈三角形框的石刻板，框内雕龙和凤的形象。

Rectangular stone slad carved with a design of beasts
Middle Warring States Period
Length 45.4cm | width 5.3cm | thickness 0.4cm
Unearthed from a Zhongshan noble's tomb No.3, Pingshan County, Shijiazhuang City, Hebei Province
Collected by the Cultural Relics Institute of Hebei Province

兽纹石刻板

Stone slab carved with a design of beasts
Middle Warring States Period
Length 14.8cm | width 12.5cm | thickness 0.4cm
Unearthed from a Zhongshan noble's tomb No.3, Pingshan County, Shijiazhuang City, Hebei Province
Collected by the Cultural Relics Institute of Hebei Province

::战国中期
::长14.8厘米::宽12.5厘米::厚0.4厘米
::河北省石家庄市平山县中山王族3号墓出土
::河北省文物研究所藏

◎ 青石板，浮雕饕餮纹和夔龙纹，图案上下对称。夔龙作回首躬身状，长尾上卷，满身饰鱼鳞纹。以夔龙对称卷曲的身尾形成饕餮的眼、鼻等。阴刻线条遒劲流畅，充满活力。

兽纹石刻板

Stone slab carved with a design of beasts
Middle Warring States Period
Length 14.8cm | width 11.4cm
Unearthed from a Zhongshan noble's tomb No.3, Pingshan County, Shijiazhuang City, Hebei Province
Collected by the Cultural Relics Institute of Hebei Province

::战国中期
::长14.8厘米::宽11.4厘米
::河北省石家庄市平山县中山王族3号墓出土
::河北省文物研究所藏

◎ 青石，局部经烧呈橘黄色。石板上浮雕四条蟠螭形兽，两两相对。四肢兽均有双形尾，身体呈「S」形弯曲。其中两只有四爪，另两只有三爪，身刻鳞片纹。身刻细斜线形条纹。动物形象弯绕曲迴，线条遒劲流畅，充满活力。

「文有（友）」四足边黄玉环

::战国中期
::长径5.7厘米 :: 短径4.8厘米 :: 内径1.9厘米 :: 厚0.35厘米
::河北省石家庄市平山县中山王䤾墓出土
::河北省文物研究所藏

◎ 黄玉制，黄中稍透青色，质纯而软，闪蜡光，半透明。环外缘的下侧有二短足，相对上侧有二耳。无纹饰，一面有墨书「文有（友）」二字。《论语·颜渊》：「君子以文会友，以友辅仁。」可能即是其字之意。

Topaz *Huan* ring with the inscription "*Wen You*"

Middle Warring States Period
Long diameter 5.7cm | short diameter 4.8cm | inner diameter 1.9cm | thickness 0.35cm
Unearthed from the Tomb of King Cuo of the Zhongshan State, Pingshan County, Shijiazhuang City, Hebei Province
Collected by the Cultural Relics Institute of Hebei Province

Dark jade *Huan* ring with inscription "*Wen Jun*"

Middle Warring States Period
Outer diameter 6.2cm | inner diameter 2.7cm | thickness 0.3cm
Unearthed from the Tomb of King Cuo of the Zhongshan State, Pingshan County, Shijiazhuang City, Hebei Province
Collected by the Cultural Relics Institute of Hebei Province

「文君」宽边墨玉环

战国中期
外径6.2厘米∷内径2.7厘米∷厚0.3厘米
河北省石家庄市平山县中山王䯅墓出土
河北省文物研究所藏

出土于西库。宽边素面。墨玉制，灰色，有黑斑，局部半透明。一面有墨书「文君」二字。

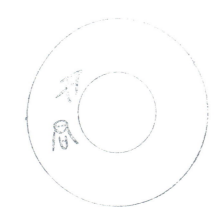

蝉形玉饰

Jade cicada shaped ornaments
Middle Warring States Period
Length 2.2~2.5cm
Unearthed from a Zhongshan noble's tomb No.3, Pingshan County, Shijiazhuang City, Hebei Province
Collected by the Cultural Relics Institute of Hebei Province

::战国中期
::长2.2~2.5厘米
::河北省石家庄市平山县中山王族3号墓出土
::河北省文物研究所藏

玉蝉为近三角形，一种青玉质，一种白玉质。蝉头部左右两凸睛，颈部阴刻两道直线，背中部起脊棱，直通头尾。脊上有穿孔。

Dark jade frog-like beasts

Middle Warring States Period
Length 1.9~2.1cm
Unearthed from the Tomb of King Cuo of the Zhongshan State, Pingshan County, Shijiazhuang City, Hebei Province
Collected by the Cultural Relics Institute of Hebei Province

蛙形墨玉兽

::战国中期
::长1.9~2.1厘米
::河北省石家庄市平山县中山王䰸墓出土
::河北省文物研究所藏

共出土17件，出土于椁室内。小兽均为墨玉雕制，蛙形，但身后有尾，上曲的尾巴紧贴臀部。兽头较扁，鼻子和眉毛横竖相接，鼻子较宽，眼睛细长，兔耳。一只只小兽昂首蹲伏，憨态可掬，意趣横生。

错银铜双翼神兽

::战国中期
::长40厘米∷高24厘米∷重10.7千克
::长40厘米∷高24.4厘米∷重11千克
::河北省石家庄市平山县中山王䜣墓出土
::河北省文物研究所藏

Bronze winged beasts inlaid with a silver design

Middle Warring States Period
Length 40cm | height 24cm | weight 10.7kg
Length 40cm | height 24.4cm | weight 11kg
Unearthed from the Tomb of King Cuo of the Zhongshan State, Pingshan County, Shijiazhuang City, Hebei Province
Collected by the Cultural Relics Institute of Hebei Province

◎ 共出土2对4件，2件出土于东库，2件出土于西库。神兽怒目圆睁，张口伸舌，獠牙外露，圆颈挺立，昂首斜向一侧，仿佛在嘶吼。前胸宽阔低垂，四肢弓曲，利爪怒张，两翼斜直向上，显得十分矫健。神兽的口、眼、耳、鼻、羽毛等处均错银线，周身错银卷云纹千变万化，背部以银错出蜷曲于云中的鸟纹。DK:36腹底铸有与DK:35同样铭文，但末尾多一『冢』字。双翼神兽形象似狮非狮，矫健有力，刻画细腻。可能作为镇器，压在席之边角，或作为陈设品以增强王之雄威。标本DK:35，腹底横铸：『十四祀，右使车（库），啬夫郭痊，工疥，冢（重）。』共13字。

错银镶金铜牺尊

::战国中期
::长40厘米 :: 高28厘米 :: 最宽16厘米
::河北省石家庄市平山县中山成公墓出土
::河北省文物研究所藏

◎出土一对。尊之造型为一小兽。四短腿直立，兽首前伸，双耳斜直，一双圆目，口微张。颈部戴项圈。小兽胸肌丰满，腹部浑圆，腿部粗壮。兽口为流。背上有活钮盖，盖钮为一只天鹅回首叼啄背上的羽毛的形态。项圈上镶包金泡饰，兽身满饰银和红铜错出的花纹，多处镶嵌绿松石。

Bronze *Xizun* wine vessel inlaid with a silver and gold design
Middle Warring States Period
Length 40cm | height 28cm | maximum width 16cm
Unearthed from the Tomb of Duke Cheng of the Zhongshan State, Pingshan County, Shijiazhuang City, Hebei Province
Collected by the Cultural Relics Institute of Hebei Province

错金银四龙四凤铜方案座

- 战国中期
- 通高36.2厘米
- 河北省石家庄市平山县中山王䰯墓出土
- 河北省文物研究所藏

Bronze square table stand decorated with dragons and phoenixes
Middle Warring States Period
Height 36.2cm
Unearthed from the Tomb of King Cuo of the Zhongshan State, Pingshan County, Shijiazhuang City, Hebei Province
Collected by the Cultural Relics Institute of Hebei Province

案是古代的小桌。此案的案面已朽，仅存案座。方案的底盘为圆形，由两雄两雌的四只梅花鹿承托。底盘之上昂首挺立四条双翼双尾的神龙，龙的双尾两侧环绕，反勾住头上的双角；双翼在中央聚合成半球形，龙尾连接处探出四只引颈长鸣的展翅凤鸟。整体造型动静结合，疏密得当，龙飞凤舞，新颖奇特。方案上的错金银纹饰精巧繁密，流畅斑斓。四条龙的龙头分别托起一件二升式的斗拱，斗拱托起案框，斗拱的形式按照当时木构建筑的挑檐结构制成，是我国最早发现的战国时期斗拱应用实例。案框一侧有铭文：「十四祀，右使车（库），啬夫郭癀，工疥。」

错金银四龙四凤铜方案座出土图

中山国大事记

前770年，白狄族鲜虞部建都于新市（今河北省正定县新城铺）。
前506年，"中山"之名首见于典籍《春秋》。
前457年，晋国灭中山国。
前414年，中山武公立中山国，建都于顾（今河北省定州境内）。
前407年，魏国占领中山国。
前380年前后，中山桓公复国，建都灵寿（今河北省平山县三汲乡）。
前327年，中山国君䶮继位，国力渐达鼎盛。
前323年，中山国与韩国、赵国、魏国、燕国共同称王。
前296年，赵国灭中山国。

司马迁的《史记·赵世家》记载

赵献侯十年（丁卯，前414年），中山武公立中山国。
赵烈侯元年（癸酉，前408年），魏文侯伐中山，使太子击守之。
赵敬侯十年（甲辰，前377年），与中山战于房子。
赵敬侯十一年（乙巳，前376年），伐中山，又战于中人。
赵成侯六年（壬子，前369年），中山筑长城。
赵武灵王十七年（壬子，前309年），王出九门，为野台，以望齐、中山之境。
赵武灵王十九年（甲寅，前307年），春正月，大朝信宫。召肥义与议天下，
五日而毕。王北略中山之地，至于房子。
赵武灵王二十年（乙卯，前306年），王略中山，至宁葭；两略胡地，至榆中。
赵武灵王二十一年（丙辰，前305年），攻中山。赵诏为右军，许钧为左军，
公子章为中军，王并将之。牛翦将军骑赵希并将胡、代。赵与之陉，合军曲阳，
攻取丹丘、华阳、鸱之塞。王军取鄗（今河北柏乡县北）、石邑、封龙、东垣。
中山献四邑合，王许之，罢兵。
赵武灵王二十三年（戊午，前303年），攻中山。
赵武灵王二十六年（辛酉，前300年），复攻中山。
赵惠文王三年（乙丑，前296年），灭中山，迁其王于肤施。

附录："神秘王国——古中山国历史文化展"展览设计图

Renderings of the Exhibition "The Mysterious Zhongshan State: Its History and Culture"

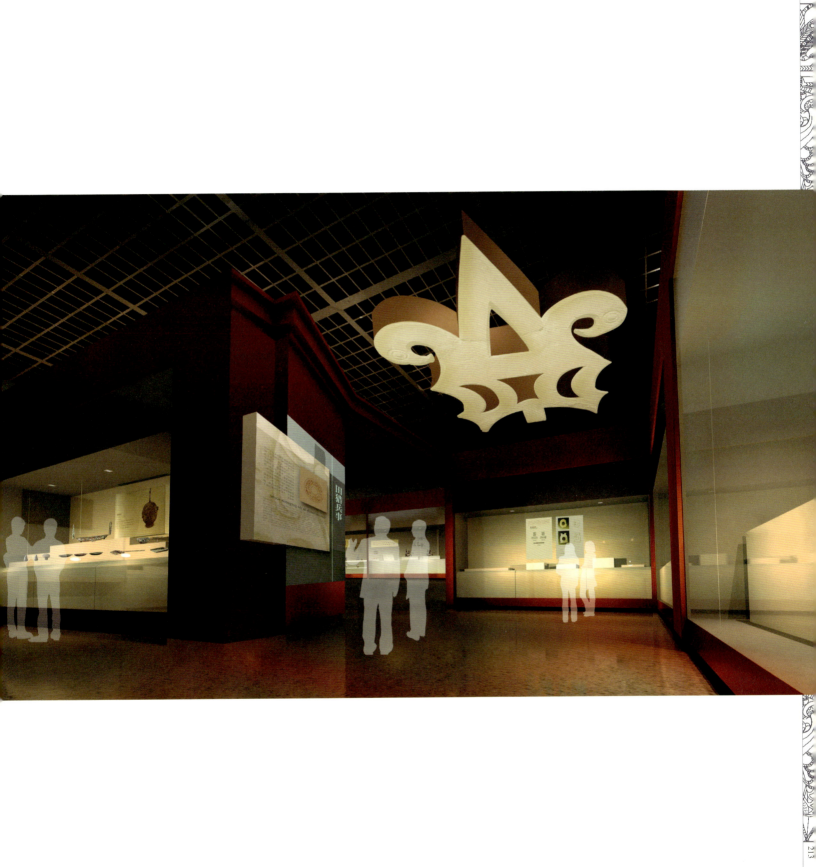

神秘王国——古中山国历史文化展

后记

为了集中展现东周时期中山文化的内涵及特点，展示中山国多年的考古和研究成果，秦始皇帝陵博物院携手河北博物院、河北省文物研究所，举办了"神秘王国——古中山国历史文化展"，并配合展览出版了同名图录。本次展览和图录集中展示了中山国的200多件精品文物，是秦始皇帝陵博物院"东周时期地域文化系列展"的又一力作。

展览是一项复杂的系统工程，涉及的工作内容非常庞杂，离不开所有参与者的努力和付出。

秦始皇帝陵博物院院长侯宁彬提出了举办中山国展览的意向，并要求相关部门积极落实；院长助理郭向东在展览具体实施过程中给予了大力支持，使展览得以成功举办、图录得以顺利出版；陈列展览部副主任邵文斌积极进行沟通、协调，并在各方面上严格把关，使各项工作有条不紊地进行；陈列展览部张宁通过收集大量文献、考古资料，撰写了展览陈列内容方案和图录文稿；陈列展览部蔡一阳完成了展览的陈列形式设计；社会教育部韩东红编写了讲解词，并对展览讲解员进行了培训；藏品管理部马生涛主任、郑宁顺利完成展品的运输工作；还有院里许多部门的领导和同事，为展览的成功举办尽职尽力、通力合作，有力地保证了展览的进度和质量。

展览图录的编撰，参考了大量专家学者的研究成果，并得到了很多同行的帮助和指导。河北博物院陈列部张丽敏主任在策划展览和图录出版中给予了宝贵的建议；河北博物院陈列部陈宁博士对此展在筹展、构思和方案撰写等诸多方面给予了大量的建议，并提供大量的文物信息和图片资料；河北博物院研究员刘卫华和河北省文物研究所副研究员孔玉倩为图录撰写了学术论文使图录增色不少；西北大学历史学院田旭东教授、河北博物院刘卫华研究员对图录稿件进行了仔细审阅，提出了非常中肯的建议；曾任职于苏格兰国家博物馆亚洲部策展人的Shiona Airlie细心审译了陈列方案、文物说明。秦始皇帝陵博物院科研规划部孔利宁完成了展览和图录的翻译、英文校对工作；赵震对图录中照片的后期处理给予了指导性建议；陈列展览部邵文斌、张宁、叶晔，考古工作部付建等几位同志认真完成了展览内容和图录文稿的校对工作。

展览得以顺利开展，图录得以顺利出版，离不开大家的辛勤付出，感谢你们！

编者

2017年6月

图书在版编目（CIP）数据

神秘王国：古中山国历史文化展 / 侯宁彬主编；秦始皇帝陵博物院编. -- 西安：西北大学出版社，2017.6
ISBN 978-7-5604-4063-7

Ⅰ. ①神… Ⅱ. ①侯… ②秦… Ⅲ. ①古城遗址（考古）-出土文物-介绍-河北-战国时代 Ⅳ. ①K878

中国版本图书馆CIP数据核字(2017)第139196号

神秘王国
——古中山国历史文化展

编　　者	秦始皇帝陵博物院
主　　编	侯宁彬
责任编辑	郭学功　琚婕
装帧设计	雅昌设计中心·北京
出版发行	西北大学出版社
地　　址	西安市太白北路229号西北大学内
电　　话	(029) 88302621　88302590
邮政编码	710069
印　　刷	北京雅昌艺术印刷有限公司
开　　本	965mm×635mm　1/8
印　　张	27.75
字　　数	200千字
版　　次	2017年6月第1版
印　　次	2017年6月第1次印刷
印　　数	1—1000
标准书号	ISBN 978-7-5604-4063-7
定　　价	360.00元
网　　址	http://nwupress.nwu.edu.cn